Crossroads

Crossroads

times of decision for people of God

Herbert O'Driscoll

The Seabury Press * New York

1982
The Seabury Press
815 Second Avenue
New York, N.Y. 10017

Cover design by
Saskia Walther

Typesetting by
Jay Tee Graphics Ltd.

Cover illustration: *Abraham,*
by Pietro Annigoni, courtesy of
Miller Services

Printed in Canada

Library of Congress Cataloging in Publication Data

O'Driscoll, Herbert.
Crossroads.
1. Meditations.   I. Title
BV4832.2.037   1983   242   82-10825
ISBN 0-8164-2432-2   (PBK.)

for
Paula, Deirdre,
Erin, Moira, Niall,
who share my crossroads

Contents

The Stranger

When I was a child, there was a hired man on my grand-father's farm whose name was John Brennan. I recall him vividly with the eye of a small boy. He wore a scarf tied around his neck, a cloth cap, trousers precariously held up with binder twine, and boots with great holes in them. He smoked a clay pipe. He had a heavy moustache that dripped hot brown tea as his face emerged from a great steaming mug during a break in the summer haymaking.

You have noticed even now that I like to linger with John Brennan. I loved him. I use the word as seriously as a child always uses it. There was one whole day (and you know how long a summer day is in childhood) throughout which I became John Brennan. I announced this fact upon arising, refusing all day to answer to my own name.

He would often tell me of his far travels. To this day I do not know for certain if he had ever been farther than Dublin, if indeed that far — all of seventy miles. But together we went in my imagination, and for all I know in his, to Afghanistan and Baluchistan. For some reason these are the golden roads I particularly remember.

Years later, when I was in my late teens, my uncle had to sell the farm. I was not there on the day of the auction, but I was told of it. John was by now in his eighties. He had worked on that farm since he was a young man, my grand-father and he having grown old together in what, I now realize, was the last of a centuries old feudal relationship of mutual trust and obligation. He had always lived in a small thatched cottage about half a mile from the farm. It was beside the well from which we drew our water.

The morning of the auction began a beautiful spring day, the day when a farm that had been worked by three genera-tions would pass out of the family. When the auction started, someone remarked on John's absence. In the last few years he had been able to do only very light work and only on a part time basis. So my cousin went to look for him, walking the half mile of winding narrow road with its long grassy banks and high hedges.

John was lying in the long grass as if asleep. In the way that Paul in the authorized version of the Bible describes the death of certain disciples, John had "fallen asleep." He had left the cottage to come to the auction, and something deep within him, and a loving Father above and around him, had decided that this spring day was the day for weariness to end and a great journey to begin.

It is for a particular reason that I have written about John Brennan and his importance to me. One evening as we sat together in the summer twilight, he elderly and I a child, John told me that *crossroads* (like those on the way to the nearby town) were mysterious places. He said that one always had to make a choice at the crossroads and that every choice in some way changed the pattern of one's life. That is why there is an old legend that both God and the devil are very often at the crossroads, waiting. Each tries to ensure that the choice is made which eventually, by many other roads and after many other choices, will bring the traveller to heaven or to hell. One had therefore, he told me, to be very careful at crossroads. They were good places to make the sign of the cross on oneself, as one decided on a direction.

It is difficult now to conjure up the kind of world where such a statement was not just a picturesque legend but a serious and disturbing warning. Then, for me, it was indeed a warning. Now it is changed not merely to a picturesque legend but to an image of spiritual truth.

The human spiritual journey, as we all know well, is full of crossroads. In a sense every daily choice we make is one. Yet there are points along the road where we face a choice of roads particularly significant in the shaping of all that is to come to, and from, our lives. At such a place we encounter the Stranger. This encounter may be one in which we experience intense temptation, searing challenge, exhausting struggle, even the ultimate moment we call death. The Stranger will be both outside us and within us, the face unknown to us and yet well known. The prize we struggle for at such a crossroads is our deepest and most essential self.

In the following pages I have tried to describe crossroads in the lives of certain people. Sometimes the crossroads are met at a relatively early stage in their journey and thus set the direction for all that is to come. However, sometimes the crossroads occur at a much later stage, and the particular choice can in a mysterious way express all that a person has become over a long journey already taken. There may even be, as in the lives of martyrs, crossroads at the very end of life, when the choice is made on the edge of the mysteries we call heaven and hell.

Whether the crossroads and the choice come early or late in the journey, they always bring a revealing of who and what we really are. Even by our simplest and most pedestrian choices we reveal much, thus giving livelihood to statisticians, poll takers, survey makers, computer programmers. But in deeper and more significant choosings we see something of ourselves and others, and so are immensely enriched even though at times appalled.

I cannot help but feel that this is true in a moment of encounter such as that between Jesus of Nazareth and the Phoenician woman who brings her agony to him on the Mediterranean coast road. Here too in this encounter is a salutary reminder that the Stranger at the crossroads may be disguised as a beggar. This is true in countless stories and legends, and in many lives of the saints. Such manifestations of the Stranger may, by forcing us to respond to another's need, lead us to discover levels of our own being which we have never known till that moment.

The crossroads I speak of blend mysteriously and tantalizingly into the ongoing terrain of our own spiritual journey. Such is often the way with Bible reading. Sometimes the immense significance of a choice taken is not obvious to us at that particular point in our journey. Only after many years, perhaps, can we look back across the inner geography of our life and point with the knowledge of retrospection to a meeting of roads and a choice that we can now see meant so much, where we now realize we encountered the Stranger. In such moments of precious insight we discover that the Stranger took us to the inn of that particular moment of time and, breaking bread and pouring wine with us, set us with burning hearts on the road to a Jerusalem that we have never merited but which, nevertheless, is by grace our most true and lovely home.

Some of the following chapters emerge from Holy Scripture, some from later Christian history, and some from our own day. I have set out to witness, as vividly and as accurately as possible, to a day when a particular person came to an especially significant crossroads.

What I have tried to do may seem presumptuous. It may be felt that in some cases we simply do not have a sufficiently complete setting from which to extract character, attitudes, moods, reactions. Yet both Jewish and Christian storytellers and writers have been doing this for centuries. I cannot help but think that it is possible to identify with a particular type of personality emerging from a Bible narrative even though many centuries may have gone by. Human personality with all its beauty and ugliness, above all with its wondrous complexity, does not change across the centuries. Joy, guilt, self-worth, regret, dread, depression, commitment, betrayal, ambition, and love are all eternals. Were it otherwise, all we have in the Bible would be valuable but barren information. Instead we have human beings who, in living out a relationship with God, touch us deeply and speak clearly to our human condition.

There has always been the wish to peer more closely at scripture and subsequent tradition, to fill its seeming gaps, to write lines between the sacred lines, to tell again the oft told story, to bring incidents into clearer focus. Over a long time the Jewish and Christian communities have judged this kind of writing, allowing some to remain because it has been deemed worthy for telling or teaching, dismissing other material because it is found wanting in some respect. To this long tradition I offer these scenes and attempted insights. I know that the wisdom of that same tradition will work its will on my efforts. I trust that wisdom to be finally the wisdom and winnowing of God.

Vancouver
Lent 1982

Noah

Third Millenium BC

God saw the earth and it was corrupt. And God said to Noah, "I have determined to make an end of all flesh; behold I will destroy them with the earth. Make yourself an ark of gopher wood. For behold I will bring a flood of waters upon the earth. But I will establish my covenant with you; and you shall come into the ark, you, your sons, your wife, and your son's wives with you. And of every living thing of all flesh you shall bring two of every sort into the ark to keep them alive with you."

Noah did this; he did all that God commanded him. Genesis 6.

● ● ●

In the Cathedral in Florence, from Advent 1492 to Easter 1493, Savonarola mesmerized a rich and decadent society by preaching on a single episode in scripture, the story of Noah.

It is a powerful and timeless story, and it has acted as a mirror for many societies in many moments of history, our own among them. It is the greatest apocalyptic story, its flood a vivid and threatening image of the disintegration of society and personal life as we know it. Even when the actual means of threat vary, from plague in the fourteenth century to World War in the early twentieth to environmental collapse and nuclear destruction in the late twentieth century, the flood remains an image of the all pervading threat.

The corruption and violence of human society, which in the Bible narrative draws the disgust of God, is obvious today in much of our political comment, in art, writing, and film. Noah himself, called by God to act, is each one of us, called in a drowning world to respond creatively in the face of the flood of events. The ark we decide to build may be a particular person or social structure. It may be a number of things. We may choose to invest energy in building our own personal life, or strengthening a relationship, or making a contribution to the local community or to a particular institution. What matters is that we opt for becoming an ark builder rather than allowing ourselves to become a passive victim of events.

If we alter slightly our identification with Noah, making him not our personal self but contemporary Western humanity, we are struck by some other significant aspects of the story. Noah builds an ark not for himself alone but for his extended family. The image communicates to us that, in an age such as ours, the development and strengthening of our own self is not enough for survival. We need others. We need to invest our energies and hope in ways of relationship and community.

However, as we read on in the Bible story, there is an even greater dimension to Noah's responsibility. God will not allow the doors of the ark to be closed until it is filled with other life forms. If in our day the planet itself has come to be seen as an ark, then the scripture is telling us that there can be no social, political, or economic salvation without ecological salvation. We cannot take care of ourselves and our society without taking care of the earth. There is an irony here — what many dismiss as the trendy obsession of environmentalists turns out to be something the scriptures have been advocating for nearly three thousand years!

• • •

The flat sunlit plain flowing away from the great river was a good place to own land, especially in hard and unpredictable times. Life was pleasant yet fragile, prosperous yet vulnerable. A man had to protect himself, his interests, his family, in a world that seemed to possess so much yet also seemed to be living on the edge of . . . of what? It was difficult to shape and express these fears. Was it because one could not pinpoint the elements of danger or because one did not dare to?

He thought often about this. There was too much violence, the old integrity of personal and commercial life appeared to be slipping away, even the weather worked against one's best efforts. For a long time he had felt disquiet rising in him. Although he could not define it, he realized also that he could not dispel it. More and more the feeling of impending crisis had been growing. In conversations in the marketplace or at home a vague uneasiness had begun to be expressed, a sadness. Sometimes among friends it could be heard as a spreading anxiety about the future.

Long afterward he never could recall the exact moment he decided to act. He could never explain why his action took the form it did. All he knew was that he felt directed in his actions. Perhaps too it was the assumption that if anything terrible happened, the river more than the violent land was the way out to something better. They would be safe on the river; so he had always felt.

They built according to his plans, but he had a strange feeling that the plans were not his. He recalled that the idea had come almost fully formed. The conviction that time was short, the sudden realizing that you either waited for disaster or you acted — all this had come suddenly and clearly to him. Sometimes, as they worked at the craft, there was a wild temptation to stop, to relax, to conform, to accept things as they were, to wait for things to blow over. Yet all his experience told him to press ahead, that things would not blow over. The fabric of his whole world seemed somehow to have weakened. The smell of breakdown was in the air.

Even as they built the ship, the world around them seemed to darken. He had never seen skies as continually threatening nor news as consistently depressing. The small irrigation channels dug in from the various branches of the river were already overflowing and turning the precious fields into mud. Travellers from the south brought back chilling stories of the crumbling of the coastline along the gulf.

He could not help noticing how the attitude of his sons and their families had changed from assistance motivated by duty to eager involvement. What had been his private nightmare, respected only because of his age and seniority, had now become a shared reality. Their world was changing, swiftly, brutally, catastrophically. He could not help thinking how impossible it was to save yourself alone. The craft was a community venture. They would need each other, and — so he passionately believed — God had need of them all.

He realized now why some directing voice had cautioned him to build generously. Each day there moved about the village groups of animals fleeing from the rising water level, animals that normally didn't trespass on human ground. Even the winged creatures risked a nearer approach in their misery and hunger. Noah and his family sometimes shared their dwindling food supply and began to select some of the finer animals, placing them on board. They noticed how the higher parts of the unfinished craft had become resting places for birds.

The day they left they had a sense of terrible finality. The communities around them had already disappeared, each one following their leaders to supposedly safer higher country. They let the craft swing out into the swiftly rushing tributary and headed for the great river itself. Once out there, they knew they had no choice. They were at the mercy of forces now gone rampant.

The old man watched day by day as they voyaged far from everything familiar. His enduring strength lay in his utter conviction that, although they had long lost any choice of direction, there was somewhere ahead a land prepared by a power greater even than the maelstrom now seething around them on every side.

He felt a deep sense of stewardship about this little earth they had built. In a disintegrating world he had been called to decide and to act. He had responded not to fear but to a mysterious call. He felt it no accident that the lives on board formed an embryonic world. The day one of the birds came back with a green leaf dried by air and sunlight, Noah knew that God had a future for the tiny earth that trembled and tossed under his feet. He smiled as he considered the satisfaction of one day soon lighting a fire on that first land they would surely come to. It would be, he thought, a great fire, a sacred fire. In its rising flames they would offer one of the animals. They would take the best animal. They would invoke the God who was Lord of their totally unkown future. Noah trusted that God would respond.

Abraham

Seventeenth century BC

After these things God tested Abraham, and said to him, "Abraham!" And he said, "Here am I." He said, "Take your son, your only son Isaac, whom you love, and go to the land of Moriah, and offer him there as a burnt offering upon one of the mountains of which I shall tell you." So Abraham rose early in the morning, saddled his ass, and took two of his young men with him, and his son Isaac; and he cut the wood for the burnt offering, and arose and went to the place of which God had told him. On the third day Abraham lifted up his eyes and saw the place afar off. Then Abraham said to his young men, "Stay here with the ass; I and the lad will go yonder and worship, and come again to you." And Abraham took the wood for the burnt offering, and laid it on Isaac his son; and he took in his hand the fire and the knife. So they went both of them together. And Isaac said to his father Abraham, "My father!" And he said, "Here am I, my son." He said, "Behold, the fire and the wood; but where is the lamb for a burnt offering?" Abraham said, "God will provide himself the lamb for a burnt offering, my son." So they went both of them together.

When they came to the place of which God had told him, Abraham built an altar there, and laid the wood in order, and bound Isaac his son, and laid him on the altar, upon the wood. Then Abraham put forth his hand, and took the knife to slay his son. But the angel of the Lord called to him from heaven, and said, "Abraham, Abraham!" And he said, "Here am I." He said, "Do not lay your hand on the lad or do anything to him; for now I know that you fear God, seeing you have not withheld your son, your only son, from me." And Abraham lifted up his eyes and looked, and behold, behind him was a ram, caught in a thicket by his horns; and Abraham went and took the ram, and offered it up as a burnt offering instead of his son. So Abraham called the name of *that place The Lord will provide; as it is said to this day, "On the mount of the Lord it shall be provided."* Genesis 22:1–14.

• • •

The city of Hebron holds Arab and Jew in an uneasy tension that sometimes collapses in bloodshed and gunfire. Lying south of Jerusalem, its streets are sometimes full of the produce of the rich high farmlands nearby. At its heart is the huge castlelike structure built by the skill and labour of a score of generations from different cultures and political regimes.

On entering its towering walls, one walks through the worlds of Byzantium and the Crusades, the world of both Mameluke and Ottoman Turk. Inside one finds mosque and synogogue. The faithful of both ancient traditions mingle with Christian pilgrims around the cenotaphs venerated by all three.

If one kneels on the floor one can see far below, dimly visible through an iron grating, the glistening rock face of the Cave of Machpelah. To do this is to look back through time at ground made sacred nearly three millenia ago. Here below one's feet Abraham, historical patriarch of three of the world's great religions, laid the body of his wife Sarah. Somewhere in the shadows far below lies the dust of those whose lives founded the most sacred traditions of untold millions to come.

The story of Abraham and Sarah, restless adventurous survivors that they were, is a story about relationships, first of a man and a woman, then of them both with the Holy One, El, the mystery we call God. Out of this long ago experience emerges an archetype of our human wrestling and journeying with God.

It is no accident that Abraham and Sarah are in almost continuous journeying. They are also on a journey with each other and within themselves. Their relationship acquires a mellow resilience and good humour; each grows and matures spiritually. The opportunistic entrepreneur who crosses the Nile into Egypt and uses his wife as attractive protective colouring for survival is not the spiritual giant who heartbrokenly prepares to make the ultimate sacrifice of his child.

One day this episode would come to prefigure for Christians an offering made by another child of Abraham, a terrible offering made on a cross looming far in the future of that long ago world of the patriarchs.

• • •

Many times he had bitterly regretted the decision to leave the prosperity and loveliness of the mountains. He had grown up in Haran and had played as a child by the familiar river that flowed south to join the great Euphrates. In turn that wide stream flowed into the gulf which in legend had flooded the world of his forefathers.

There had been Sarah of course. She had always been with him, always the loving if sometimes formidable wife. He sometimes wondered where true authority had often been, where the source of strength had really lain — in his manhood or in Sarah's womanhood. Perhaps it was in both. He realized now that she had taken a great deal over the years. On more than one occasion she had agreed to masquerade as his sister, to barter her body so that he would be spared a midnight knife between the ribs to dispatch an inconvenient husband. She had loved him in spite of their childlessness. She had come to deal with the shame and frustration of it by making light of the whole thing. He never forgot the day her laughter died away before the disturbing gaze of the visitor who had come to them, in their old age, to tell them with a terrible and quiet authority that they would have a son. It was strange how he had simply refused to believe it, perhaps because there already was a boy to continue his name, Hagar's son Ishmael. How Sarah had detested that girl and her boy!

One thing had never dimmed since he had led them all

down from the northern hills of Haran, down the valley of the smaller southern rivers to the dangerous Canaanite territories. There had always been a sense of destiny. He had never managed to be any more precise about it than that, but the sense of it had always remained strong. It had often served him well in situations where steady nerve and morale were essential. In the corridors of power on the Nile where one wrong move would have been disastrous, in dealing with the seething hordes of tribesmen in the awful dust-filled oven of the Jordan valley, in the dangerous foray he had made far into hostile territory to get back his nephew Lot — in all these moments a sense of being called had made all the difference.

The thought of Lot brought back the memory of places now only deserted ruins, skeletal and ghostly in a sea of solidifying ash. He had always known Sodom and Gomorrah's glittering decadent world would come to a bad end. He had hoped that good leadership could bring reform. He still believed that it only needed a few of the right kind to make a big difference. He smiled at his long ago hopes, marvelling at his own presumption in bargaining with God.

It was strange, he thought, how real God had always been to him. There were men who felt insecure outside their own familiar valley, the home of their particular god. Yet to him, God had seemed as near in Beer-sheba on the edge of the desert as in far away Dan where the Jordan rose. In the valley or high on the hills, resting in a fortified town or waiting under the stars for morning to come — always there had been a Presence, quiet yet insistent. He had heard it address him as a voice deep within his thoughts and emotions.

There had been times when that sense of relationship had been terribly tested. Above all he remembered the time of ultimate testing. Perhaps in everyone's life there comes a self-questioning about the quality of one's own faith. Abraham recalled that strange and terrible day when he seemed to move trancelike toward a dreaded but unavoidable rendezvous. In the end God asks each one of us to give back what we most prize, whether it be our deepest love, our most passionately lived life, our most treasured possession. Perhaps in the mystery we call death we in turn receive both love and life given to us with a richness and loveliness as yet beyond our imagination. Was this what God had been trying to teach him that dreadful day when the pyre had been laid and he stood with the knife drawn above the body of his son, avoiding the child's eyes as he tried through blinding tears to discern the face of a demanding God in the blue vault of heaven?

He looked out now beyond the opening of the great black tent, beyond the brow of this hill called Hebron. Even now from the bed of his old age he could see the flocks on the slopes. Beyond the grazing area was the rocky outcrop where Sarah's body had been laid so many long years ago. There had of course been many other women. Life had given him much — power, influence, respect. But Sarah had given him devotion. What was it he had dreamed one night under the desert stars as he ran the sand through his fingers? Descendants, the dream had shown him, descendants as many as the stars in the sky and as the grains of sand.

Although the old man knew that this promise had already been made again to his son Isaac, he could not imagine how it could ever be. He now found that he simply trusted it would be so. In the long love affair he had had with God, Abraham had come to find God trustworthy.

Jacob

Sixteenth century BC

And Jacob sent messengers before him to Esau his brother in the land of Seir, the country of Edom, instructing them, "Thus you shall say to my lord Esau: Thus says your servant Jacob, 'I have sojourned with Laban, and stayed until now; and I have oxen, asses, flocks, menservants, and maidservants; and I have sent to tell my lord, in order that I may find favor in your sight.' "

And the messengers returned to Jacob, saying, "We came to your brother Esau, and he is coming to meet you, and four hundred men with him." Then Jacob was greatly afraid and distressed.

The same night he arose and took his two wives, his two maids, and his eleven children, and crossed the ford of the Jabbock. He took them and sent them across the stream, and likewise everything that he had. And Jacob was left alone; and a man wrestled with him until the breaking of the day. When the man saw that he did not prevail against Jacob, he touched the hollow of his thigh; and Jacob's thigh was put out of joint as he wrestled with him. Then he said, "Let me go, for the day is breaking." But Jacob said, "I will not let you go, unless you bless me." And he said to him, "What is your name?" And he said, "Jacob." Then he said, "Your name shall no more be called Jacob, but Israel, for you have striven with God and with men, and have prevailed." Then Jacob asked him, "Tell me, I pray, your name." But he said, "Why is it that you ask my name?" And there he blessed him. So Jacob called the name of the place Peniel, saying, "For I have seen God face to face, and yet my life is preserved." The sun rose upon him as he passed Penuel, limping because of his thigh. Genesis 32:3–7, 22–31.

● ● ●

When Sir Arthur Quiller Couch, then holding the august

chair of English at Oxford, was commenting on the story of Jacob and Esau, he made a remark so quintessentially English that it deserves immortality. He said that the difference between Jacob and Esau lay in the simple fact that Esau was a gentleman and Jacob was not. After we have had our smile, we may find the remark as good a description of this great story as any.

Jacob and Esau are brothers and very unlike each other. In their youth Jacob betrays his brother by deceiving their aged and blind father Isaac. Jacob accepts from his father's hand the blessing that is Esau's birthright as the older son. From that moment Jacob is a fugitive from Esau. However, he is above all a survivor. At the outset of his flight he dreams one night of a great ladder set up between earth and heaven. He hears God reaffirming to him the promise made to his grandfather Abraham.

There follow years of wandering, mainly in the area of Haran in northern Syria where his grandfather Abraham had come from. Jacob accumulates great property while proving himself even more canny than his father-in-law Laban. Into his life comes the lovely Rachel and, as was the fashion of those days, many other women. From this man, and from the extraordinary mixture of human gifts and faults that he embodies, will come the family whose names will identify the twelve tribes of Israel. The very word *Israel* is in fact another name of this strangely fascinating yet unattractive hero.

Jacob is an example of the willingness of God to use what seems unpromising material for the divine purposes. As with Abraham we are introduced to no lily-white and noble hero. We meet a very ordinary human being. As that human being journeys hither and yon, we watch him grow, mature, deepen. Sometimes this process is one of great pain, sometimes it is actually the stuff of laughter. As the laughter of Sarah and Abraham at an unlikely pregnancy echoes down the centuries, so we laugh at the struggles of Laban and Jacob as each tries to score against the other.

For Jacob there was always a shadow over life. The guilty

memory of his wrong to Esau never faded. He knew that it would have to be faced some day. There came the day when Jacob was told that Esau was coming north with four hundred men. . .

● ● ●

They had spent most of the day getting what seemed an endless caravan safely down the slope from the high plateau. At this point the river they would have to cross, the Jabbok, ran through a deep gorge on its way west to where it joined the Jordan about ten miles further on. By day the steep walls of the gorge held the heat; by night they threw long black shadows that frightened both men and beasts.

It was common and ancient knowledge that every river valley held the dark spirits of the river who were free to emerge at night but forced to disappear at dawn. Jacob knew he could not keep the caravan in this threatening place for the night. He brought together the headmen and gave them his orders. They were to assemble the whole caravan so that it moved ahead in very precise order at dawn. The forward scouts had informed him that Esau was coming north from Seir and was only a day or two away. The dreaded encounter had to be well stage managed. Above all he had to impress, he had to give the appearance of success, of strength. All his life his guilt had robbed him of self-esteem, even as he had become more and more self-confident. He thought of himself as small, Esau as large. Now it was essential that his possessions and achievements give him the stature he could never himself feel.

There was no particular moment when he had planned to be alone. He suddenly found himself making the decision when the caravan leaders came to report that everything was now safely across the river and camp was pitched on the other side. Only the immediate family remained on the northern bank. Before his resolution wavered he ordered Rachel and Leah and the other women to go with the men. He watched them disappear into the gathering darkness. For a while he heard the sounds of their passage; then he was alone, the only sounds the crackling of the fire and beyond it, in the darkness, the roar of the river. The world seemed to have become enclosed by the cliff faces around him. He had become the single inhabitant of a tiny shadowed universe.

At some moment between the coming of night and the first light of dawn, Jacob discovered that this dark universe was shared by another. The face that seemed to hang suspended in the darkness was strangely both familiar and unfamiliar, the voice a whisper yet also a thunder. At first he felt paralysed with fear. All the stories of a desert childhood screamed and gibbered in his imagination. Yet there was about this appearance a substance and a dignity, a kind of majesty beyond the scampering bestial demons of his superstitions.

The vision held him for awhile until he felt a sudden longing to struggle free. There flooded through him an energy he had not felt for years, a mingling of rich emotions he had long forgotten. Rage, fear, even a fierce joy, an exulting in the struggle filled his whole being. Time itself seemed to quicken as they swayed back and forth in the darkness. The struggle drew from him powers he had not realized he possessed. He heard himself shout his effort and exultation. Sometimes the shouts seemed to become screams as his assailant thrust and struck at him.

Suddenly the struggle ceased. He felt a terrible lassitude pass through him. There was a sudden searing pain in one leg. Through waves of pain he heard himself crying out a denial of his very name. He felt the self he had hated for so long being taken away and, in its place, an indescribable and blessed sense of being renewed. Desperately he called out for the being with whom he had wrestled. He became aware of the first light of dawn in the line of sky above the gorge. Beside him the fire embers were black on the sand. The river sang its way to the Jordan. The world itself seemed somehow refashioned. There was an inexplicable yet undeniable sense of his whole inner world having changed. Perhaps he couldn't define it now, perhaps he never would fully understand. One thing above all he believed with a new found passion. He had in that terrible darkness seen the very face of God. He had felt the hands of God upon him forming him anew in pain and struggle. And he knew, as humanity has come to know, that when we dare to approach the face of God, the divine light exposes our inmost self. Then it is either our own will or God's will for us that conquers, either annihilation or purification. Even now, as he limped into the river, Jacob felt its coolness cleansing and revitalizing. He walked from the water and began to climb the side of the gorge; dawn broke across the desert.

Jacob could see the encampment nearby. Everything had been prepared as he had ordered. Far in the haze of the new day, figures were approaching. He knew this would be Esau and his company. When they met, the brothers embraced and wept. As Jacob looked into his brother's eyes, he felt for a moment that he was seeing again the eyes that had gazed at him in the darkness of the night. The memory lasted for a moment and chilled him; then Jacob felt it fade, blotted out by an affection and acceptance he had never been able to accord to himself but now saw, where he had never thought to see it, in the eyes and voice of his brother Esau.

Moses

Thirteenth century BC

Now a man from the house of Levi went and took to wife a daughter of Levi. The woman conceived and bore a son; and when she saw that he was a goodly child, she hid him three months. And when she could hide him no longer she took for him a basket made of bulrushes, and daubed it with bitumen and pitch; and she put the child in it and placed it among the reeds at the river's brink. And his sister stood at a distance, to know what would be done to him. Now the daughter of Pharaoh came down to bathe at the river, and her maidens walked beside the river; she saw the basket among the reeds and sent her maid to fetch it. When she opened it she saw the child; and lo, the babe was crying. She took pity on him and said, "This is one of the Hebrews' children." Then his sister said to Pharaoh's daughter, "Shall I go and call you a nurse from the Hebrew women to nurse the child for you?" And Pharaoh's daughter said to her, "Go." So the girl went and called the child's mother. And Pharaoh's daughter said to her, "Take this child away, and nurse him for me, and I will give you your wages." So the woman took the child and nursed him. And the child grew, and she brought him to Pharaoh's daughter, and he became her son; and she named him Moses, for she said, "Because I drew him out of the water."

One day, when Moses had grown up, he went out to his people and looked on their burdens; and he saw an Egyptian beating a Hebrew, one of his people. He looked this way and that, and seeing no one he killed the Egyptian and hid him in the sand, Exodus 2:1–12.

• • •

The story of Moses is one of the great extended biographies of the Bible. It abounds in high moments of achievement. In a word from our own time it is Churchillian. Before it ends, a great empire has been successfully challenged, a potential nation has been created, one of the world's most formative spiritual encounters has been experienced. And perhaps the greatest achievement of all — a demoralized and disunited rabble have been moved through the most appalling terrain, their morale kept high in spite of frequent disasters and their own volatile nature. Although most of those who had streamed east from the lowlands of the Nile delta were destined to grow old and die in the brutal geography of the Sinai and the Negev, the genius of Moses managed to keep alive the vision of a new land.

In the circumstances of those wilderness years there must have been moments when, on any human level, the probability of gaining that new land seemed extremely remote. As one follows their tortuous and troubled migration, one is aware of moments when only the finest quality of leadership could have prevailed over their wish to return to the known slavery of Egypt rather than face the unknown terrors of heat, thirst, volcanic disturbance and, with the passage of time, enemies that lay ahead of them.

Yet face these things they did. We can only presume that two elements became fused to create their steel-like resolution. One was the personal conviction of Moses that he was an instrument of the God of history, chosen to form at least a chapter of that history. The other was the Sinai encounter, forever mysterious and majestic, by which a whole people felt themselves forged together as an historical and moral instrument of a God whose name they would hesitate to speak but whose love they would be incapable of finally ever setting aside.

As one reads the book of Exodus, it becomes possible to be present on an actual day when a choice was made, a choice that led to the formation of a people and became the means by which the civilization we so easily take for granted received the timeless moral concepts that would make possible much of the human story as we know it.

• • •

He had asked the driver of the chariot to wait for him at a distance. The driver, also bodyguard, was obviously unhappy about the order but had no choice except to obey. It was probable, Moses thought bitterly, that the driver would be duty bound to report his request, first to go into this particular part of Goshen, and secondly to enter the area of the delta where the brick making went on. It was rarely that any chariot other than those of the guards was seen in this place. There was really no particular reason for any Egyptian to come here. The area was far from the northern cities, most people didn't understand the guttural language of the Hebrew slaves, and there was a general unwillingness in palace circles to do otherwise than acknowledge their existence.

He moved over to where one of the square kilns stood. For some reason, it was not in use, and he was able to vault up on to the wall. This gave him a slightly higher vantage point to look over the area where work was going ahead. The kilns stood in lines along the river bank; around each one worked a group of slaves. Other slaves were at work forming the delta mud into the endless supply of bricks for the gleaming walls of temples, pyramids, palaces, and storehouses that he would return to in a few hours.

Moses realized that by coming here at all he made himself vulnerable. The court of Pharaoh was a hotbed of political rivalry. There seemed to be a power struggle brewing. There was also a nervousness, real or manufactured, about the Hebrews. They had bred like flies. Even though they were weaponless and always under scrutiny, there was a sense of their being somehow a threat. He wondered if this vague mixture of fear and hate was the reason for his own sense of insecurity. His mother had never hidden his own origins from him. But years of exclusive court upbringing had detached him from any sense of identification with this shambling filthy horde who now lived to serve his kind and society.

All that was until recently. Now he didn't know why, but

he was drawn here by something deeper than he so far could understand. Even as he stood on the wall he could hear the occasional shout of a guard, followed by the crack of a whip on a bare back and the cry of the slave.

It was such a sound that now alerted him. This time it didn't end in a single cry. The whip lashed again and again. His eyes searched the area to pinpoint the incident. Feeling strangely a spectator to his own emotions, he was amazed at the sudden choking rage that welled up inside him. He could now see the little knot of activity. It was almost hidden by another of the kilns. He scrambled to the ground, and in a moment he was running. As he approached the group, the slaves parted to let him past. They were amazed and even frightened at his appearance.

Suddenly he was aware of the brutal face of the guard who had straightened up from the prostrate figure on the ground. The expression was already changing from cruel authority to fawning respect. The slave on the ground was trying to crawl away. Moses could see the flies already settling on the bleeding back. A terrible rage swept through him as he took in the scene, a rage that terrified and mystified him even as it took possession of him. The guard's face seemed to float in a red mist suffused in the pitiless sun. There came a blood lust and rage that second by second began to peel away layers of his deepest being. He felt himself drowning in this terrible passion. Like a drowning man, he saw his life played out before him. Memories — a woman's face and body; was it his nurse or his mother? The great river itself, a sense of another long ago drowning. Songs heard as a boy from elderly servants in the palaces, songs of the desert, songs of a God beyond all the gods. Those songs rose to a great timeless cry, lonely and wild and terrible. Then there was silence.

Afterward, long afterward it seemed, he had vague memories of standing there as the slaves handed him back the blood stained spear, of their frantically dragging the body into the shelter of the kiln wall and covering it with sand, leaving him alone, trembling like a leaf, desperately trying to

recapture his composure before walking back to the mercifully distant chariot and its escort.

As he walked slowly he knew that nothing would ever be
the same again. A god utterly demanding and revealing had
entered him. This God could enter a soul, and could embrace
a human being in a passion and purpose beyond imagining.
He had not realized such a powerful God existed. In all the
pantheon of Egypt Moses could find no name for such a God.
He knew only that all was changed, changed utterly.

David

About 1010–970 BC

Three of the thirty chief men went down to the rock to David at the cave of Adullam, when the army of Philistines was encamped in the valley of Rephaim. David was then in the stronghold; and the garrison of the Philistines was then at Bethlehem. And David said longingly, "O that some one would give me water to drink from the well of Bethlehem which is by the gate!" Then the three mighty men broke through the camp of the Philistines, and drew water out of the well of Bethlehem which was by the gate, and took and brought it to David. But David would not drink of it; he poured it out to the Lord, and said, "Far be it from me before my God that I should do this. Shall I drink the lifeblood of these men? For at the risk of their lives they brought it." Therefore he would not drink it. These things did the three mighty men. 1 Chronicles 11:15-19.

• • •

David is the Old Testament hero above all others. However, to be an Old Testament hero is not always an enviable role. Those who wrote the ancient scrolls had an extraordinary determination to be realistic even about those whom they wished to remember as heroic. We see this in both Old and New Testament lives. In spite of the fact that by the time the gospels were written the apostles' place in the community was very high, there is no hesitation in the writers to relate incidents that are not to the credit of the twelve. We have only to think of the clumsiness of the request of James and John for high places in the expected kingdom!

Many biblical characters come to us in short vignettes. Particular aspects of their personalities are remembered, particular incidents in which they were involved. Many men and women are mentioned only by name, walking for one moment onto the stage, sometimes uttering one line in the script, remaining only a face in a crowd. In David's case we are brought face to face with one of the giants of biblical history. The amount of material we have to work with is comparable to the amount we have about Abraham and Moses.

In such biblical characters we have enough to allow a personality to emerge. First we see David the achieving youngest son. With Jonathan son of Saul he becomes the young warrior with easy access to high places. Next David becomes the guerilla leader, showing the charisma that throughout his life drew to him men and women alike. Scene by scene we are taken through his years of kingship. He continues to be the charismatic leader and shows himself a superb strategist; he builds an empire which his people will never again equal and which in a single generation his son Solomon will squander away.

All the time there is another David, a femininity complementing the masculinity, a poet hidden in the warrior, a passion behind the calculation. His dancing naked before the public procession of the ark, the affair with Bathsheba — these moments reveal the sensualist who also appears in the rich language of the psalms.

Above all, the hero shows his feet of clay in the cynical betrayal of Uriah, a loyal officer but husband of the woman David is determined to possess. The writer makes no excuses, softens nothing. Yet by a peculiar alchemy seen sometimes in history, it is this very quality of human fault that rounds out the heroic portrait. In our own experience virtue may spark a relationship, but the mutual acceptance of fault will deepen it. A similar unpredictability marks our attitude to public figures. In one person a single fault draws our contempt; in another the subtle mix of qualities is enhanced by a fault revealed. Among some lines of Shakespeare put into the mouth of Antony about Brutus, there is a phrase

> The elements so mixed in him
> That nature might stand up to all the world
> And say this was a man.

• • •

From where he stood he could hear the general chit-chat of the men. They sat lounging in the shadow of the rock face. Every one of them he knew intimately. He knew the gifts they had, mainly for killing with extreme and enthusiastic efficiency. Without them he could never have got to this point. Only a few months ago they had together achieved the impossible. Under darkness they had come by night along the Kidron brook to look up at the watch-fires of the Jebusites blazing on the walls built atop the huge granite ridge. He had found where a narrow funnel cut in the rock led from the valley floor into the heart of the citadel. He shuddered now as he remembered the long climb in pitch darkness, the fight to suppress waves of claustrophobia that threatened to unman him. But there came the moment of emerging into an empty courtyard, the whispered commands, the sudden shouting of his own name as a battle cry, the screams. By morning the citadel was theirs.

If he lived forever, he would not forget standing on the walls in the light of dawn. The night's work had left him intoxicated with a mingled euphoria and bone weariness. There were moments when the hills and the battlemented walls seemed to flow into one another, melting and shimmering in the rising sun, until the tiny crude citadel seemed to flow beyond him, spreading to other hills, many towered, graced with a golden splendour. He smiled as he recalled waking in the shade of one of the rooms. They had found him by the wall sprawled in a sleep of total exhaustion. He gathered that Eleazor had carried him there and left him to rest while they got on with the grim business of consolidating the take over.

That had all been months ago. Already the citadel had partially become his in the village round about. They were beginning to call it "David's city," and in a way he found difficult to express he too felt an affinity with it. The dreams he had had that first morning would, he knew, come true. Capturing Jerusalem somehow had set the seal on the anointing they had given him in Hebron a few months before.

It was Eleazor who interrupted his thoughts. Left to himself he dreamed too much. He was always amazed that these incredibly tough guerilla fighters stuck with him. It was an alliance of opposites in so many ways. Yet he could, if he had to, kill with the rest of them, and for that matter take his women better than any of them. It was a strange joke of God, he thought, to link so closely the things of love and the things of death.

Eleazor's call was to supper. They gathered, beginning to discuss the campaign. Jerusalem was far from being an ending of the fighting. There was still the matter of Philistine power. At this very moment the Philistine army group was only a few miles away in the valley of Rephain south of Jerusalem, while another detachment of theirs had surrounded the hill village of Bethlehem only seventeen miles away from where he lay. David knew the Philistines of old. He had a continuing love-hate relationship with them. He had lived in their cities, even once feigned madness to escape being butchered. He had marched with them, used them, fought them, made alliances with them when it suited both of them, engaged in mutual betrayals when expedient. They had always, he realized now, completely understood one another. Either he would rule them or they would kill him. At least some issues in life are mercifully clean cut.

The talk moved into planning. The question was, When next should they strike? Various possibilities were discussed, sunset gave way to nightfall, the flames leaped higher, and cloaks were thrown on. At one stage David reached for a goatskin filled from a nearby stream, tried to drink, spewed the water from him in disgust, and wished aloud that he could again have a decent drink from the clean shimmering depths of the well by the gate in Bethlehem. At the time no one said anything. He thought no more of it.

Morning came. He emerged from the cave shadows to the smell of food. There was a stir among the men, a quieting that made him curious. From behind the group came Eleazor carrying a goatskin. With him were Ishbosheth and Shammah. All looked bone weary but somehow pleased with themselves. Eleazor offered him the goatskin, gestured him to have a drink. Puzzled but playing along David lifted the soft heaving sack to his lips. At the last moment he hesitated and let it drop again. Experience had taught him that leadership was subtle, it could never entirely blend with friendships however deep. He asked peremptorily what the goatskin held. There was a moment's hesitation. They too understood the unspoken subtleties of their relationship with him. They too had watched the anointing at Hebron. They told him of the decision to go over the hill pathways, slip through the Philistine lines, fill the skin at the well. Yes, there had been a couple of guards, but that was expected and easily dealt with. They grinned and suggested that David drink.

He stood there dumbfounded. The remark about wishing for a drink had been so casual, yet three of them had risked life to get it for him. He stood for a moment and his eyes began to fill. He silently damned his own weakness for displaying emotion. When he felt he could keep his voice steady, he refused to drink. He realized what he would do. He walked over to the nearby tiny stone altar erected by some long ago occupant of the cave. Raising his voice he offered the contents of the skin to God, naming it as beyond price since life had been risked for it. The clean stream spilled from the neck, spread into a flood, shattered the morning sun for David's eyes into a thousand flashing jewels. It splashed from the rock drenching him as it fell, before running into the dust and the stones.

They never forgot the moment. Years later they still recalled it. After he and they were long dead, it would be remembered as a moment when all the elements so mixed in

David came together in a gesture of tenderness and sensitivity acted out on the edge of brutality and slaughter, a moment of purity among obscenities, love among lusts, friendship amid killing. It would be a moment in which David would stand for ever surrounded by the eternal ambiguities that mingle in every man as high heroism and base humanity.

Herod

The Great King, 73 BC–4 BC

Now when Jesus was born in Bethlehem of Judea in the days of Herod the king, behold, wise men from the East came to Jerusalem, saying, "Where is he who has been born king of the Jews? For we have seen his star in the East, and have come to worship him." When Herod the king heard this, he was troubled, and all Jerusalem with him.

Then Herod summoned the wise men secretly and ascertained from them what time the star appeared; and he sent them to Bethlehem, saying, "Go and search diligently for the child, and when you have found him bring me word, that I too may come and worship him." When they had heard the king they went their way; and lo, the star which they had seen in the East went before them, till it came to rest over the place where the child was. And being warned in a dream not to return to Herod, they departed to their own country by another way.

Now when they had departed, behold, an angel of the Lord appeared to Joseph in a dream and said, "Rise, take the child and his mother, and flee to Egypt, and remain there till I tell you; for Herod is about to search for the child, to destroy him."

Then Herod, when he saw that he had been tricked by the wise men, was in a furious rage, and he sent and killed all the male children in Bethlehem and in all that region who were two years old or under, according to the time which he had ascertained from the wise men. Matthew 2:1-16.

• • •

His name is synonymous with villainy. Shakespeare has Hamlet warn an actor not to "out-Herod Herod," meaning he is not to rant and threaten and generally be what the theatre calls a "heavy." Herod's memory has become so tainted in

Christian memory that it is easy to forget he held the title Herod the Great.

Actually Christian memory has tended to merge no less than six Herods together. The reason is that almost every one of the six is linked with a confrontation of some kind. Herod the Great is forever linked with the slaughter of children in Bethlehem. His son Herod Archelaus reigned in Judea when Mary and Joseph skirted that area on their way back from Egypt. Another son Herod Antipas imprisoned John the Baptist and had him butchered. That same man taunted Jesus as our Lord moved through the trials before his crucifixion. The fourth Herod, another son Philip, was ruling the Caesarea Philippi area when Jesus visited there with his disciples. A fifth Herod, Agrippa I, is mentioned by Luke as a persecutor of Christians and as having later died horribly. Finally a sixth Herod, Agrippa's son of the same name, met Paul before the apostle set out on the long voyage to Rome. It is only at this point, about AD 60, that the name Herod begins to gain some respect in the New Testament.

Herod the Great was an Idumean who became king of the Jews under the umbrella of Roman power. He was an extraordinarily gifted man. His family connections with the great commercial houses of Petra, coupled with his lifelong friendship with Mark Antony, placed him at the centre of world events of that time. He transformed Jerusalem into one of the ancient world's magnificent cities. The temple that Jesus knew was then just completed after more than thirty years building. Six city blocks long, higher at its pinnacles than the later great Gothic cathedrals of Europe, it shone blindingly white in the Palestine sun.

In old age Herod's life sank into depravity and cruelty. Members of his own family died under his growing paranoia. In the year of our Lord's birth Herod had visited the Dead Sea to try to ease the agony of his disease ridden body. Half crazed by fear, deluded and threatened by every possibility, the question of the visiting Persian magi provoked a predictable response. Herod's palace fortress was only a few miles from Bethlehem. From here the troops rode to slaughter a generation of the village. Within the year the same road up the mountain would see the magnificent procession that had set out from Jericho. At least four regiments marched; there were 500 servants carrying spices. They climbed the mountain to the marble stairway. Herod's body lay on a golden bier in full royal array covered with gems. He would have approved. He probably planned every detail.

• • •

From where he lay, wishing for sleep so that he could be at his best on the morrow, he could see the harbour far below, the citadel gleaming in the moonlight, his own ship at anchor in the inner harbour, its torches flickering at bow and stern.

He had taken care to pace the journey from Jerusalem as meticulously as possible, embarking at Joppa for the voyage to Rhodes, deliberately not coming into the harbour until this morning, the day before the all important meeting with Octavian. Everything had to be orchestrated as harmoniously as possible. Herod was under no illusions. In this coming interview he had only to handle Octavian wrongly and not only would his political career be at an end but quite possibly his life.

Unable to sleep Herod began to think about the events of recent months. He sometimes wondered how significant this last year had really been. Would it be looked back upon some day as one of the extraordinary hinge periods in history where actions were taken and decisions made that would bear consequences far beyond their own particular moment. Mark Antony was dead and so was Cleopatra. Both had been guests in his house on more than one occasion. Antony he had known for years since Herod had been sixteen and the young Roman officer twenty-six. Cleopatra he had always detested and had made no secret of his opinion to Antony. In spite of Herod's warnings Antony had remained totally infatuated with the Egyptian queen. In the end, after the terrible disaster at Actium (it was hard to believe the battle had been fought only the previous September), Antony had realized that the game was up. Octavian was now master of the Empire and had been singularly unimpressed by the Egyptian queen in whose arms both Antony and Julius Caesar had lain. Seeing the cold eyes of the thirty-two year old Octavian, Cleopatra had with typical realism proceeded to end her life.

It was before the battle of Actium that Herod had made the decision not to help Antony directly. Friendship had nearly drawn him to Antony's side. A mutual friend Alexas had arrived with the appeal. The ironic result was that Herod had convinced Alexas to get out while there was time, to leave Antony. Hatred of Cleopatra and, in the end, contempt for Antony's inability to see her as his destroyer, had kept Herod from sending the much needed reinforcements. He wondered now if Octavian was fully aware of this. It could be very useful tomorrow in the fateful interview.

Herod reflected that he need not have come to Rhodes at this particular moment. He could conceivably have waited for Octavian to come to Palestine. Octavian was nothing if not thorough. Step by step the eastern provinces were being visited, loyalties were being examined, political debts were being paid, retribution was being meted out with savage efficiency, new alliances made. Herod knew the whole process intimately.

He was surprised at himself in the morning. He had slept well. He realized there was something in his nature that enjoyed even this knife-edge gamble. The consummate actor in him rehearsed the scene. He recalled afterwards that as usual he had intuitively judged his audience well. He had long ago decided on his strategy, working it out on the slow October voyage from Palestine. There was no point in trying to fool Octavian. Herod and he had met before, and Herod knew his man. He would speak of the situation exactly as it was, tell Octavian of his year's long friendship with Antony, fully admit his frequent support of Antony as a friend. All this would have to be laid on the table for the very simple reason that Octavian would be well aware of every detail.

All this went through Herod's mind as he dressed. Again and again he analyzed his approach for flaws. Deliberately he put aside the gold circlet he would normally have worn about his head. Instead he would carry it to use at the right moment if things were going as he hoped. He went through the streets of Samos in his own chariot, escorted by his own soldiers. Octavian was waiting. Pleasantries spoken were not reflected in the Roman's eyes. Herod knew that he was playing for his life.

He played magnificently, moving through a script that for once had the advantage and simplicity of truth. He hid nothing. He did not beg or whine or bribe. He had shared in and sorrowed for Antony's defeat. For that reason he was not wearing his crown in the presence of Octavian who had vanquished Antony. With a slight hesitation Herod threw all on a single dice. "All I ask of you Octavian," he said, "is that you consider not whose friend, but what a good friend, I was." With that he stopped and stepped back. He knew that he might be spending his last day as a free man, perhaps his last day on earth.

The cold eyes looked at him. Herod could almost feel them analyzing, balancing possibilities, deciding his future. At last Octavian pointed toward the gold circlet between them on the floor. He motioned to Herod to pick it up and put it on. Herod knew that he had won.

He had more than won. There followed reinstatement, assurance of Senate ratification of his throne. Within a few months he and Octavian, having landed from Rhodes at Acre, were riding south together in military escort along the coast road.

The visit to Rhodes, the ability to throw that terrible dice of life and death, showed in Herod what would eventually earn him the title "the Great." It was to prove typical of him to decide to face Octavian instead of waiting for fate to overtake him. It was not the first nor would it be the last time

Herod would show his decisiveness. Thirty years away in the future, old and hideously ill, he would respond to another threat. He would fear for the stability of his power because of the birth of an unkown child. It would trigger in Herod swift and savage reaction. Ironically by that decision, brutal but by the norms of his day realistic, he would inscribe his name on history far more indelibly than the name of Octavian, who had held Herod's life in his hand yet whose power would fade into insignificance in the light of that sought for child.

Jesus
of Nazareth

And Jesus went away from there and withdrew to the district of Tyre and Sidon. And behold, a Canaanite woman from that region came out and cried, "Have mercy on me, O Lord, Son of David; my daughter is severely possessed by a demon." But he did not answer her a word. And his disciples came and begged him, saying, "Send her away, for she is crying after us." He answered, "I was sent only to the lost sheep of the house of Israel." But she came and knelt before him, saying, "Lord, help me." And he answered, "It is not fair to take the children's bread and throw it to the dogs." She said, "Yes, Lord, yet even the dogs eat the crumbs that fall from their masters' table." Then Jesus answered her, "O woman, great is your faith! Be it done for you as you desire." And her daughter was healed instantly.

And Jesus went on from there and passed along the Sea of Galilee. And he went up on the mountain, and sat down there. Matthew 15, 21–29.

● ● ●

I hesitate to include in a series of chapters such as this a particular moment of decision from the life of our Lord. The main reason for my hesitation is the very fact that for a Christian he is always Lord. For the Christian, Jesus of Nazareth cannot be one of a series. He stands uniquely alone.

On the other hand, our Lord lived a fully human life. However, this statement must always be placed in the context of the mystery of divinity in humanity in Christ, which constitutes the central and eternal mystery of the Christian faith. No mental and verbal struggles to express this are going to prevent it remaining a mystery till time ends. Even then I suspect that the mystery, rather than being explained, will become the heart of a further revelation totally beyond my present imagining.

However, because Jesus comes to me as a man, born and living and dying in a particular time and place, as I must, knowing (so the faith teaches me) all the elements of my humanity, then I am driven to conclude that he shares with me all the elements of life as a progression of experience.

Did he then at times and for certain reasons regret a past action such as, let us say, inviting Judas into the circle of disciples? Did he have to decide from moment to moment courses of action, responses to challenges? Did he sometimes wish that he could have access to a glimpse of the future to see consequences of present decisions? Did he sometimes have doubts about his own thoughts and actions? Were some relationships in his life more or less difficult than others? Above all, to ask a question asked frequently since the middle of the nineteenth century, did he know who he was? I realize that to frame the question so directly may be over-simplifying an issue that is forever irresolvable. Though this may well be true, the question is asked in this straightforward way by millions of thoughtful Christians.

My own answer to these questions is to say Yes to all of them. For if any of these experiences is missing from the life of Jesus of Nazareth, then his presence among us was other than fully human. By acknowledging this I deny nothing of that mysterious quality we call divinity.

The encounter we are going to reflect upon was, I have always felt, a key moment in our Lord's growth, both in self-understanding and in the dimensions of his mission. My effort to enter into this particular encounter in his life and to assume certain consequences that flowed from it, is written with a prayer that it is understood as neither limiting nor diminishing Jesus of Nazareth as Christ and Saviour.

● ● ●

The journey from the lakeside goes uphill from Capernaum

and across the rolling countryside of Galilee. As always there comes a moment when the air changes and the sea is not far off.

When they came down from the hills again they could see the city of Tyre in the distance, walled toward the east where it faced the mountains, the stone arms of the harbour reaching out to the gleaming smooth Mediterranean. This was the farthest they had ever moved from the familiar inland lake surrounded by its towns. The experience was both exciting and a little unnerving. Also they were now in Syria, out of Herod's jurisdiction. Somehow one felt a little more vulnerable on this foreign soil. The fact that they had seen an occasional platoon of Roman legionnaires moving through the countryside served to remind them of the empire whose symbols remained constant whether the soil was Galilean or Syrian.

They were not quite sure why Jesus had come so far. Their surmise from the odd remark dropped was that the demands had become so great around the lakeshore communities that he felt the only solution was to get totally away. He sounded and looked drained and preoccupied. For most of the journey there had been almost no discussion, as if he was deliberately remaining within himself.

It was therefore a subdued and anxious group who noticed the woman approach as they rested. The fact that she had been following in the distance for a while had only prompted the dry ribald suggestion that she was some enterprising whore from a nearby village. She had called out to them earlier in the day, and they had ignored her. Jesus himself seemed oblivious to the incident. But now she came near. They noticed that she was tired and distraught. From her dress they knew she was a Canaanite, most probably local. They were unprepared for the sudden intensity she brought. Ignoring them she stood on the edge of the group and spoke to Jesus who was lying a short distance away. When she addressed him as Son of David, they realized how far the news of him had spread. Her appeal was for a daughter.

The demon she named was all too familiar to them all. They had agonized in helplessness many times over the sudden terrible spasms, the withdrawn tongue, the deathlike coma, friends or relatives beseeching them or Jesus to do something.

He gave no sign of having heard. They weren't quite sure whether it was exhaustion or a determination to remain uninvolved. She continued to call until he stirred. His being wakened annoyed them, and they expressed it. She backed away a little but rallied. Seeing him awake she again told him of the epileptic child. By now he was sitting up facing her as she came near and stood over him. Once again they heard him attempt to distance himself, although kindly. He explained that as a Jew he was of one world and she of another. Her response was to drop to her knees. The words "help me" whispered urgently brought her oppressively close to him. The imposition may have triggered a momentary impatience. He was short. The image he used was severe. He reminded her of the custom of wiping hands at a dinner table on the bread offered for that purpose, the crumbs then falling to be eaten by the house dogs. There was no doubt where she was assigned. To the disciples listening the sharpness of the retort was a measure of his tiredness.

As they watched she recovered from the barb, hesitated, and then made a decision. She looked at him, and mustering an immense and extraordinary dignity said simply that, if those were the humiliating terms she must accept on behalf of her child, then she would gladly accept them. There was absolute silence. In the distance a thin bugle call lifted for a moment on the breeze, singing of the huge worlds of empire and power far beyond their own tiny world. In the stillness they could see his eyes looking at her. He was now alert, and she seemed to engage his awareness totally for the first time.

As he spoke, all weariness seemed to slip from him. With each word the tone grew richer and stronger. Still talking he scrambled to his feet, taking her hand, lifting her. All of them could sense his deep emotion as he expressed wonder at the quality of her faith and love. He then spoke of her child as already cured. When he had ceased, she turned without a word and walked by them. She never looked back as she disappeared over the rim of the hill. No one spoke. Jesus was looking away west to where the late afternoon sun shimmered and danced on the sea binding the endless empire together. His gaze seemed to probe vast distances as if their significance was realized in a new way.

Days afterwards, far inland from the sea on a hillside above the familiar lake, they saw him looking at the vast crowd that had gathered. They could see its variety of people. Most were local, but there were others, hundreds of others — Greek merchants, Syrian traders, Roman local administrators, merchants on their way through from Aden and Egypt and from the far away endless mountain ranges of Persia. Somehow the disciples realized they were looking at a world far larger than any they had hitherto considered. In some mysterious way the world seemed to have come to him. It seemed that all people and times and places now passed within the reach of his healing power. They looked at him with new eyes, and some of them recalled the woman who had shown them the possibility of a larger believing world.

Nicodemus

Politician

Now there was a man of the Pharisees, named Nicodemus, a ruler of the Jews. This man came to Jesus by night and said to him, "Rabbi, we know that you are a teacher come from God; for no one can do these signs that you do, unless God is with him." Jesus answered him, "Truly, truly, I say to you, unless one is born anew, he cannot see the kingdom of God." Nicodemus said to him, "How can a man be born when he is old? Can he enter a second time into his mother's womb and be born?" Jesus answered, "Truly, truly, I say to you, unless one is born of water and the Spirit, he cannot enter the kingdom of God. That which is born of the flesh is flesh, and that which is born of the Spirit is spirit. Do not marvel that I said to you, 'You must be born anew.' The wind blows where it wills, and you hear the sound of it, but you do not know whence it comes or whither it goes; so it is with every one who is born of the Spirit." Nicodemus said to him, "How can this be?" Jesus answered him, "Are you a teacher of Israel, and yet you do not understand this?" John 3:1–10

• • •

The part played by Nicodemus in the life of Jesus of Nazareth is precisely that — a part in the play of events.

Nicodemus appears three times in the Gospel according to Saint John, and there is an intriguing progression to his entries. John first brings him on stage near the beginning of Jesus' public ministry, next when threatening questions were being asked in high places about this teacher from Galilee, finally when nothing seems to remain except a corpse waiting for burial. This progression provides a dramatic unity to what we know of Nicodemus. It would not be difficult to frame a three act drama around it. To use only the criterion of courage, we can see Nicodemus emerging each time from what we might call the studied anonymity that social prominence almost always desires and cultivates.

His first encounter was somewhere near Jerusalem. Since we know that Jesus used the Bethany home of Mary and Martha and Lazarus, there is at least a likelihood that the meeting took place there. However, if it did, there must have been real trust on the part of Nicodemus that neither Jesus nor his hosts would embarrass him by making the visit common knowledge. This time he comes because he is curiously intrigued by what he sees and hears.

The next time we meet him is in very different circumstances. We are in no village but in the heart of the city. We are in the Sanhedrin, the corridors of power, where much is at stake. Power can lift careers very high, and it can shatter them very swiftly. In spite of this, when intense disapproval of the Galilean is being voiced, Nicodemus risks his career by pleading for at least a fair hearing.

Finally we meet this courageous yet tentative man when the tragedy has actually occurred. It is the evening of a Friday of crucifixion. More courageous and less tentative, Joseph of Arimathea is ready to give a tomb out of respect for the dead teacher. As evening falls Joseph finds himself joined by an unexpected and prominent companion. Nicodemus, still haunted by that late hour conversation of some years before, comes to bury in the tomb what he continues to seek for at the deepest level of his being.

• • •

In his position obvious contact with the Galilean would be imprudent. He thought at one point of forgetting the whole thing. It would make life unnecessarily complicated, and God knows in such complex and sensitive times wise men did not stir up what could be left undisturbed. But such was his inner turmoil that he could not let it rest.

In the end he settled for a careful approach, sending one of his household to make an arrangement with one of the Galilean's followers. Even then he had to be careful to preserve the dignity of his own rank and office. Members of the Sanhedrin did not beg audience of wandering Galilean teachers. Yet to demand an audience, especially to demand that this Jesus of Nazareth come to him, somehow seemed wrong. When Nicodemus reflected on this he found to his surprise that he could not help but accord the man a measure of authority that strangely eradicated the difference that lay between them in social rank.

In the end the arrangement was made. By his own request the meeting had to take place out of the public eye. The suggestion came back that he might consider inventing some reason to go to the nearby village of Bethany, stay overnight, and in the late evening meet in a certain designated house where the Galilean stayed from time to time.

There were moments on the afternoon journey and throughout the early evening hours when he very nearly changed his mind. Something quite undefinable held him to the appointment, and after sunset he left the simple inn in Bethany, where he had had his evening meal, and proceeded carefully through the narrow streets until he came to the house.

There were four people — the Galilean, another man, two women. Sensitive to the moment, the Galilean made no introductions. At his suggestion he and Nicodemus moved outside and climbed the stairs to sit on the sweet smelling palm branches strewn on the roof top. Here they could speak quietly and privately.

Nicodemus became terribly conscious of the paradox of it all. He was aware that by some alchemy the situation was not under his accustomed control. In an effort to regain control he began over-fulsomely to put this rural visitor to Jerusalem at his ease. As soon as he spoke he knew that he had been clumsy. What came back to him pierced through all the conversational game-playing.

I tell you,
unless a man has been born over again,
he cannot see the kingdom of God.

Because it also pierced to the heart of his longing, it was somehow free of hurt. It summed up all the dreams of something better, something different, dreams that engage the mind in the myriad duties and complexities and compromises of daily public life.

The shaft was so well aimed that he tried to deflect it by wit. It had served him well on many occasions. Here it did not. Again the quiet voice cut through the half-hearted defences of his tired sophistication.

No one can enter the kingdom of God
without being born of water and spirit.
The wind blows;
you hear the sound.
You do not know where it comes from,
where it is going;
so with everyone who is born of the spirit.

Nicodemus felt a strange mingling of hurt and joy. Was it possible to be lashed yet to find oneself longing for the stern discipline of that quiet tongue. All pretense was now gone. Instead there came a question heavy with longing: "How is this possible?" It was cried out from such depths within him that the Galilean signed him to quietness. Nicodemus realized that he had wanted so often to express a longing for the possibility of something better. He had wanted to express it in boring committee meetings, at cynical dinner parties, on empty and meaningless public occasions. His face was working now in the moonlight, his eyes glistening with emotions longing to be released, his body leaning forward as if thirsty to drink at a well discovered in a desert place.

The voice of Jesus kept its steel edge as it addressed him in the silence. "What! is this famous teacher of Israel ignorant of such things?"

It was a knife slicing away at the very heart of his self-image. Nicodemus thought of the library in his house — the expensive scrolls, the endless study to be considered worthy of his prominent position, the contempt felt sometimes for the unlettered, the superiority gained by possession of the latest *bon mot* from Rome or Athens. There seemed now to be a hollowness about it all. Beside this the quiet Galilean seemed to have placed a haunting alternative, haunting because of its being at once unreal and yet totally real, a kingdom shining and beckoning in the deepest level of his being yet mysteriously beyond and outside him. Nicodemus was aware of something that terrified him in its certainty. He knew that this figure, half hidden in the sweet smelling darkness, had only to ask him and he would follow to the world's end. His soul cried out for the invitation yet shrunk from it in terror.

He found himself at the bottom of the stairs peering for direction in the darkness. He knew that there would be no sleep. Many hours later some shepherds crouching at their small fire noticed the pacing figure and invited him to share their circle. They were amazed that a man so dressed should sit and eat with them. Soon after dawn he left them and headed in the direction of the city.

Peter

Fisherman, Apostle

And as Peter was below in the courtyard, one of the maids of the high priest came; and seeing Peter warming himself, she looked at him, and said, "You also were with the Nazarene, Jesus." But he denied it, saying, "I neither know nor understand what you mean." And he went out into the gateway. And the maid saw him, and began again to say to the bystanders, "This man is one of them." But again he denied it. And after a little while again the bystanders said to Peter, "Certainly you are one of them; for you are a Galilean." But he began to invoke a curse on himself and to swear, "I do not know this man of whom you speak."

And immediately the cock crowed a second time. And Peter remembered how Jesus had said to him, "Before the cock crows twice, you will deny me three times." And he broke down and wept. Mark 14: 66–72.

● ● ●

He stands from first to last at centre stage in the New Testament drama. We meet him at the quayside in Capernaum. We bid farewell to him as we read his two letters to the scattered Christian communities throughout the empire. In the material we have about Peter the most obvious quality he displays is a capacity for growth. One aspect of this is his ability to recover after personal failure. Peter is immensely resilient.

The very first moment Jesus encounters him, or at least decides to approach him to gain his allegiance (for they may well have encountered each other before in that small lakeshore world), Jesus senses this quality of resilience. In that moment Simon gets the nickname by which he will become immortal. "Peter" is of course simply *petrus*, the Latin word for a rock, which is precisely what this man was to become in ways beyond his friends' wildest imaginings in the early days of their friendship. Yet there is always in Peter's life the utterly contrasting strengths and weaknesses.

He becomes one of the inner three among the disciples, yet it is he who on the mountain of Transfiguration blurts out the one response that is quite wrong. The very nature of the mountain-top experience is that it cannot be clung to.

It is Peter who answers Jesus in the pagan environs of Caesarea Philippi, the sparkling source of the Jordan being background to their conversation, when Jesus asks them the all important question, "Who do you say I am?" Into the silence Peter makes his great profession. Yet in a few minutes he earns Jesus' rebuke for questioning the decision to go to Jerusalem.

It is Peter who denies Jesus, yet who does so precisely for survival at that moment. It is Peter who has the great liberalizing vision about things clean and unclean, which releases the early church to consider the Gentile mission, yet it is also Peter who compromises on this very issue and earns the lash of Paul's anger. How many millions down the ages and in our own day will like Peter zealously affirm the Christ and, to maintain an imagined security, will also compromise their faith.

Our final contact with him is the two great letters — mature, compassionate, calm. Their tone is sombre and realistic, and yet they are full of a gentle shared strength.

We shall probably wonder to the end of time exactly where and how and when he died. A very early and strong tradition points to Rome and to the year AD 64. It tells of Peter's wish that, if he was to die by crucifixion, he be hanged upside down, since he was not worthy to hang as his beloved Lord did. The tradition rings true to the man as we know him.

● ● ●

He realized that, while the possibility of tragedy had

sometimes crossed his mind, he had not really believed it would happen. Tension had certainly been building for days, but he had put some of it down to the normal edginess they all felt on a visit to Jerusalem. All of them except Judas were lakeside men. They felt trapped in the labyrinth of narrow city streets. Peter had a suspicion that this particular week their movements as a group had been carefully watched. Even more ominous had been a new tension in Jesus that could be almost physically felt. They had never seen him act as he did soon after coming into Jerusalem. Peter had been appalled, partly at the consequences he knew could flow from the attack on the temple money exchange, but he realized now that he had never seen the depth of blazing indignation and contempt that Jesus had displayed in the few moments during the incident. As nothing else could, it made him realize that something essential had changed. This was hardly the Jesus who had asked men and women newly healed to refrain from telling others of his healing gifts.

From that day every word and every act had deepened the sombre mood of the group. Each evening they had dispersed to wherever they had procured lodging in the city. Most stayed at the house of Mary, whose son Mark made them feel totally welcome. They knew that Jesus had set out for Bethany where there were old friends, Lazarus and his two sisters. Each morning they had met in the temple area, and their conversation tended to be an exchange of the various items of disquieting news circulating as rumours. With characteristic bluntness Thomas maintained time and time again his first response when Jesus had announced the decision to go to Jerusalem. With bitter resignation Thomas had said, "Let's go with him so that we may die also!" It seemed now that Thomas had not been far wrong.

This terrible day had climaxed with the hour's long meal during which it became obvious that Jesus was agonizing about something. Each statement and action increased the intensity. Peter himself had been appalled at the sight of Jesus on the floor with a towel and water, so much so that they had

very nearly had an altercation. When he spoke of the bread
and the wine as being his body and his blood, they were too
stunned to do anything but comply. Peter recalled later the
hoarse whispers and moans that came through the trees of
Gethsemane from the kneeling figure. His own total exhaustion shamed him but still forced him to sleep. That same sleep
now gave a kind of dreamlike quality to the memory of all
that had happened. The sound of marching feet, the torches,
the screaming scuffle with one of the high priest's staff — he
recalled standing there shocked into immobility at the
suddenness of it all — the awful thing he had seen Judas do,
the crashing sound among the olive trees as most of the others
ran in animal fear.

The memory of the torches became for Peter the actual
flames of the fire at which he was sitting. The images of the
night focused in a face looking at him. The cheeky friendly
face of the girl was grinning, enjoying the attention she was
getting. "You were with him weren't you?" she asked, jerking
her head toward the door beyond which Jesus had been
escorted. Peter went cold for a moment with fear. Suppose a
nearby guard had heard her. He forced himself to remain
calm, to keep the denial casual and good humoured. The
danger passed. However, just in case, he decided to move
from the fire. Heading for the outer porch he saw a group of
people already there. He was trying to make a quick decision
either to continue on past them or to retreat inside again
when he heard the remark. It was directed at the group, but
he heard the words *with Jesus* quite clearly. This time he par-
ried by grinning and dismissing the accusation with a friendly
obscenity. It chilled him to apply such words to the particular
situation, but he knew it was either that or risk drawing the
attention of the group. He had already turned into the courtyard again, deciding that maybe the best cover was to stand
near the duty watch, when to his horror the group followed
him. This time there was more than one voice. Somebody
made a sneering remark about his northern accent. Peter lost
all control. Fear and tiredness together poured out of him in

anger. He made as if to attack the man who had spoken. Out of the corner of his eye he could see the guards looking curiously. He didn't care. They had taken Jesus. Perhaps the best thing was to be taken too.

Suddenly attention swung away from them all. The door opened and Peter saw the small procession emerging. Obviously another stage in the night was beginning. He nearly shouted when he saw the utter exhaustion of Jesus' face. He desperately tried to position himself quickly. Nobody was paying any attention to him now. As the squad turned down the slope of the grounds they saw each other. There was a moment of recognition as their eyes met. Peter felt as if he were drowning in great dark pools of indescribable sadness. Their eyes held until the platoon passed into a grove of trees and turned north toward the upper part of the city.

There was no point in going back into Caiaphas' courtyard. He felt also that to follow immediately was to risk further questioning. The sky was lightening to the east over the Mount of Olives. People were stirring. Somewhere lower down the slope a cock crew. The high soaring sound tore at Peter's last vestige of self-control. He remembered a moment of stupid posturing which Jesus had gently punctured by speaking of such a moment as this. It was still, thank God, too early for spectators to his misery. Crouched among the trees his body heaved in response to the agony within him. There were so many things — the gulf between the dream by the lake and the obscene turn of events in this cruel city, the endless strain of being increasingly defensive, the shock of Judas, the realization that some people were actually determined to destroy a human being of utter integrity and selflessness, above all the hatred of himself for having to deny, even for the sake of survival, that he knew Jesus. He recalled moments when he had pounded the table and announced his willingness to handle anything — prison, pain, death — anything. The waves of shame and self-condemnation poured over him. There was a moment when he even contemplated ending it all before his mind revolted from the thought. As long as Jesus needed him he would stay close by.

He awoke in the same spot to the sounds of the day. Nobody was near. He thanked God for the hardiness which life on the lake boats had given his body. He was hungry. He had to find Jesus whatever was afoot. He recalled something he had forgotten from the night before last. At the table Jesus had said to him that he, Peter, would be broken by events. Jesus had ignored his bluster and had gone on to say that when he had recovered (Peter recalled that word *when* rather than *if*) he was to strengthen the others. From the depths of experienced shame and self-condemnation can rise the determination to lead and inspire the timorous imagination. Peter realized, as he had so often before, the immense insight of this man from Nazareth.

He scrambled to his feet. He needed cold water for his face, something to eat, then he would try to get some information. He thought of scouting out the house where they had eaten. As he walked along the slope of the hill avoiding the houses, he heard some shouting. It was some distance away, further north. It sounded as if it might be from the Antonine Tower behind the temple. The procurator lived there. Peter headed in the direction of the noise.

Paul

Tentmaker, Theologian, Apostle

And the word of God increased; and the number of the disciples multiplied greatly in Jerusalem, and a great many of the priests were obedient to the faith.

And Stephen, full of grace and power, did great wonders and signs among the people. Then some of those who belonged to the synagogue of the Freedmen (as it was called), and of the Cyrenians, and of the Alexandrians, and of those from Cilicia and Asia, arose and disputed with Stephen. But they could not withstand the wisdom and the Spirit with which he spoke. Then they secretly instigated men, who said, "We have heard him speak blasphemous words against Moses and God." And they stirred up the people and the elders and the scribes, and they came upon him and seized him and brought him before the council.

And Stephen said: "Brethren and fathers, hear me . . . . " Now when they heard these things they were enraged, and they ground their teeth against him. But he, full of the Holy Spirit, gazed into heaven and saw the glory of God, and Jesus standing at the right hand of God; and he said, "Behold, I see the heavens opened, and the Son of man standing at the right hand of God." But they cried out with a loud voice and stopped their ears and rushed together upon him. Then they cast him out of the city and stoned him; and the witnesses laid down their garments at the feet of a young man named Saul. And as they were stoning Stephen, he prayed, "Lord Jesus, receive my spirit." And he knelt down and cried with a loud voice, "Lord, do not hold this sin against them." And when he had said this, he fell asleep. And Saul was consenting to his death. Acts 6:7–12; 7:2, 54–8:1.

• • •

One of the ways we can be assured that the scriptures depict real life rather than romantic fables is the frequency with which we are brought heavily down to earth.

It is Jerusalem. It is not yet a year since the events of Calvary and the tomb and Pentecost. A new movement is gaining ground and forming its communities. Its life is intense. Extraordinary incidents of healing are taking place. Emotions are high. There is an infectious excitement, a level of loyalty and courage obvious even in the face of high authority. Certain individuals such as Peter are playing roles far beyond what seemed their capacity only a few short years ago.

Yet amid all this high drama we are confronted with something that in its domesticity and ordinariness is almost laughable. Within the embryonic Christian community (the name Christian is as yet not in use) there are deep cultural differences. As the new community in Jerusalem gathers to eat together, there is resentment. Greek speaking people begin to feel that Aramaic speaking people are being favoured. The situation comes to the ears of the apostles, who impatiently wash their hands of the issue and decide to appoint seven men to look after the meals. There they will "deacon" or serve others.

Such is the pedestrian and undramatic way in which Stephen enters Christian history. The young enthusiastic deacon turns out to possess a brilliant mind, a passionate commitment to the crucified and risen Jesus, a level of courage that was to prove fatal. Confronted by those who are prepared to challenge the new movement at its birth, Stephen brings on himself the terrible force of a society fearful for its civil and ecclesiastical order. He is condemned by an absolutism as adamant as his own.

Stephen never knew it, but his death was to be linked forever with what later became almost an obsession among Christians. It would appear in many religions and cultures, and it would provide a power that would fuel vast religious and military drives. It was the phenomenon of martyrdom.

In the seventh century it would empower the cavalry of Islam; in the tenth century the knights who joined Peter the Hermit for the holy places would be driven by it. In the twentieth century it would empower Janani Louwum to face Idi Amin, and some years later it would prepare Caesar Romero to face the El Salvadorian junta in his Cathedral. Both men would die in the name of human justice, but both would be empowered to do so by the grace of Christ.

There is an ancient saying that the blood of the martyrs is the seed of the church. What is significant about Stephen's death is that there was a witness to it, a young man who stood on the edge of the crowd, blazing with the same kind of fervour as Stephen but for a diametrically opposed cause. His name was Saul, but one day it would be changed. Without either of them realizing it, they were very closely bound together.

• • •

For a young and brilliant Jew it was in more ways than one a long way from Tarsus to Jerusalem. Tarsus was an alive and exciting university city. The east-west land traffic of the empire moved through it from the Levant along the coast route to Ephesus and the Aegean. Yet Saul had always longed to live and study in Jerusalem. In Tarsus, as in any Graeco-Roman city, his Judaism was lived out as one thread in a glittering tapestry of religions and cultures and life styles. Somehow, even though this was to some extent also true of Jerusalem, there was another dimension to life here. In Jerusalem, Judaism itself was the context in which all the other elements had to fit. Here the very air and ground were Jewish. One could find one's roots here as a Jew.

Roots were becoming important to Saul's generation. If Judaism was to survive in the religious shopping arcade of the Empire, it had to become aware of itself. The last hundred years had seen a bewildering maelstrom of clashing ideas, civil revolt, wild eyed Messiahs, neurotic dreams of political grandeur. Saul felt that Judaism could ill afford any more fragmentation and frantic, if intellectually stimulating, religious enthusiasm. It was a time for conserving.

It was this very quality in him, this instinct for the conservative, that had brought him so gratifyingly to official notice. He admired the decisiveness of the tasks assigned to him. He was convinced that the communities springing from the Galilean rabbi's unfortunate if attractive record were more than a public nuisance. Left unchallenged they would be a serious threat to an already fragile status quo. The real threat, as Caiaphas intelligently saw, was that Rome would not differentiate between normal Judaism and this latest radicalism. If Rome retaliated, all would be lost under the imperial heel.

Saul found himself in total agreement. He accepted the assignment given him. He would report directly to Caiaphas. His task was to seek out the leaders of the new movement and accumulate sufficient evidence to make the arrest. After this the smaller fish could be caught at leisure. What was paramount was to nip the roots of the movement in the bud.

What saddened Saul was the quality of some who had become involved, above all, his contemporary Stephen, a mind as good as his own, a tongue just as articulate, an energy as unbounded, a determination as strong. The fact that Saul realized this made Stephen's commitment to the crucified Galilean even more incomprehensible.

The occasion which above all others enraged and exasperated Saul was Stephen's public examination. When the time came for the defence plea, the performance that Saul and others witnessed was almost flawless. The Greek in Saul would have wished for greater detachment in Stephen, a cooler head, more rationality. The Jew in him couldn't but admire the passion that erupted at particular moments. But underneath any grudging admiration for Stephen, Saul felt his own rage and contempt mounting. It was the way he heard Stephen handling history. All the facts were there. Saul could agree with all of them. Yet it was the extraordinary way in which everything was twisted slightly to make the dead Galilean the centre of events, the pivot of it all — to posit as the Messiah of Israel a common criminal bleeding on a Roman cross!

Saul suddenly found himself screaming his agreement at the death verdict. There was something here in Stephen that had to be done to death immediately, something fearful and insidious and deadly that, if not annihilated with the utmost resolve, would infiltrate and poison the world as Saul knew it.

By the time they reached the place of execution he had calmed down. The man of ideas was becoming nervous of the reality ahead. For a while he looked at Stephen in grudging admiration. Around him the more enthusiastic asked him to look after their outer cloaks while they prepared to hurl the jagged stones in a kind of sweating ecstasy. When Stephen was driven to a kneeling crouch Saul heard him give a sobbing shout. All he could hear was the word *forgive*. He looked wildly around for a way out, a way to remain yet retreat from the butchery. He realized there were some around him not taking part. He saw one man's lips moving in prayer. Suddenly his official role came to his rescue. Here was an ideal moment to identify others in the movement who had come to support Stephen in this terrible moment. Leaving the pile of coats Saul began to move through the edges of the crowd, listening, memorizing, identifying. Somewhere behind him out of sight the voice of Stephen screamed once and was silent. In Saul's mind, trying to concentrate on his task, the sound seemed to echo on and on.

Patrick

Bishop, Missionary, died AD 460

I bind unto myself today
The strong Name of the Trinity,
By invocation of the same,
The Three in One, and One in Three.

I bind this day to me for ever,
By pow'r of faith, Christ's incarnation;
His baptism in Jordan river;
His death on Cross for my salvation;
His bursting from the spiced tomb;
His riding up the heav'nly way;
His coming at the day of doom;
I bind unto myself today.

I bind unto myself today
The virtues of the starlit heaven,
The glorious sun's life-giving ray,
The whiteness of the moon at even.

Against all Satan's spells and wiles,
Against false words of heresy,
Against the knowledge that defiles,
Against the heart's idolatry
Against the wizard's evil craft
Against the death-wound and the burning,
The choking wave, the poison'd shaft,
Protect me, Christ, till thy returning.

Christ be with me, Christ within me,
Christ behind me, Christ before me,
Christ beside me, Christ to win me,
Christ to comfort and restore me,
Christ beneath me, Christ above me,
Christ in quiet, Christ in danger,
Christ in hearts of all that love me,
Christ in mouth of friend and stranger.

The Breastplate of St Patrick, from ancient Irish sources

• • •

The context for Patrick's life and work can be set by linking it with a specific event. In the spring of the year 410 Alaric the Goth rode into Rome. Twenty-two years later the small ship carrying Patrick and his companions dropped anchor in the smooth waters of Strangford Lough on the north-east coast of Ireland.

When the gates of Rome opened to Alaric and began a new age of world history, the man who would one day be remembered as Patrick was somewhere in northern Gaul studying in preparation for ordination as priest and consecration as bishop. He had one overriding desire. He was determined to return to the mist shrouded pagan island to which he had been dragged in boyhood as a slave and from which he had escaped in response to a divine vision.

His name is an adaptation of the Latin word *patricius*, which means merely "the noble one." His real name is long gone. All we know is that, by the middle point of the fifth century, the missionary work of some spiritual giant had transformed the religious life of the whole island and had brought into the Christian world a people who would embrace the faith with a passion and a creativity beyond most.

We of course can see what Patrick himself could not see.

Western Europe, particularly around the Mediterranean, was about to shatter under invasions far more brutal than that of Alaric and his Goths. The elements of Christian organization and culture in that area would look for a place of refuge. It would be found in the harsh world on the edge of Europe, the islands and coastlands against which the Atlantic surged. But when Latin Christianity turned for refuge to the north-west, it discovered a foundation already laid by Patrick's work. From AD 432 to 461 he laboured, a flame of courage and, missionary genius far from what seemed the centre of the world's stage.

Today, as one moves in a tourist pleasure cruiser down the waters of the river Shannon, one can see the mounds and stones of Clonmacnoise now silent and deserted. Here in the sixth and seventh centuries would stand a university of not less than 6,000 students from all over a darkening Europe. Such was the light that the work of Patrick had lit. Such was the light that was to create many other lights in the centuries ahead.

We meet Patrick at a moment when he had decided to penetrate the heart of Celtic power in Ireland. He is boarding a ship to sail south along the east coast for the march inland to Tara and the seat of the High King.

● ● ●

Early on Holy Monday they embarked from the stony beach which edged the western side of the lough. Patrick was still depressed from Milchu's suicide, still seeing the flames consuming the home of the man who had once enslaved him but had killed himself rather than face what he understood as the new "magic" Patrick possessed. He felt that Milchu's death freed him of an obligation. Now came a key decision. He would move toward the centre of pagan power in the island. They would go to Tara.

He had formed a strategy making it essential that they reach the religious and political centre of the island by the

Saturday night before Easter Day. The designation of the day as Easter was of course his alone. All around them older and darker gods possessed the innumerable groves and high places of the island. But he knew, from the years spent as a slave boy tending sheep on the slopes of Mount Slemish, that those older gods also dealt much in fire as a symbol. Many a time he could recall the flames leaping into the night as dusk fell and the local Druidic priests celebrated the ancient rhythm of the seasons.

They slid down Strangford Lough heading for the open sea. He had thought of heading for Tara by what was known as the northeast road, one of the five roads radiating from the High King's palace. But it ran for the most part through the endless forests that cover the island. If he were to use it, there was the danger of attack as well as the possibility of word going ahead of his coming. He needed the drama of surprise to carry out his plan.

The short voyage south, all the way within sight of the shore, was uneventful. Both nights they went ashore to sleep. Once far out to sea they saw a ship heading away from them. The seas were dangerous, and many pirate ships raided the coast of Britain now that the Roman legions had retreated.

On the third day they rounded the headland and glided into the mouth of the river Boyne, paid off the owner of the boat, and went ashore. It was Maundy Thursday. That evening they shared in a simple act of Bread and Wine before the evening meal. Early in the morning they set out along the green bank of the river. All day they walked, resting only when necessary, until toward evening they came to Ross-na-ree, the burial chambers of the kings. He knew now that Tara was very near. One of them climbed a nearby hillock and called out that he could see the buildings of Tara. They prepared for the night.

He had planned carefully for Saturday. A hilltop nearby was selected. He stood on it to check personally whether King Laoghaire's palace or *rath* could be seen. Then for hours the company of them cut branches and piled them as high as they could reach. At dusk they began the Easter liturgy, their voices rising and falling across the silent fields.

As dusk fell he found himself glancing more and more to the south-west. He knew two things. Tonight was the celebration of the spring equinox in the Druidic circle. Also Laoghaire had issued a command that under pain of death, no fire other than the sacred Druidic fire was to be lit. The moment he told one of the brothers to put a torch to the pile of wood there would be no going back.

Suddenly a distant flame broke the gathering darkness. At Patrick's gesture the torch was lit, there was a moment of catching, and then with a roar the wood blazed. Long afterward he would hear of the consternation the fire caused, the surprised king, the enraged chief Druid, demanding some men to investigate. But even while this was going on, the company of monks were already moving swiftly across the river and along the forest road. As they came to the great Hall of Assembly, they met the soldiers coming out. Patrick had dressed himself liturgically, a large wooden cross in his hand. He realized that all depended on the impression being given of confidence and complete authority.

Marching through the guards he led his men into the interior of the hall, his shadow looming high on the mud baked walls in the light of the blazing fire. From behind the High King came the Druid priest named Lochnu. He faced Patrick and loudly condemned this desecration of the gods. The two of them stood at the centre of attention, their words clearly audible. Each represented in that moment a divine power. All expected a sign as they watched. The two faced one another, Patrick speaking of the new Easter fact of Christ. Suddenly and unexpectedly Lochnu tripped on something in the long shadows around the central fire. As he almost fell there was an audible gasp. Patrick's figure seemed to loom higher for a moment and he cried, "Some trust in chariots and some in horses, but we will walk in the name of our God." It was both an expression of contempt for the fall of Lochnu and a battle cry for the newly risen God. It was the moment of decision.

In the dead silence a figure near the king detached himself and threw himself at Patrick's feet. It was Erc, son of Dego, the king's page. He demanded baptism into the fellowship of Patrick's God.

There would be much talk in the days to come. There would be a number of conversions, but the moment of Lochnu's fall and Erc's coming forward was the moment of decision. Tara, stronghold of the High King, had not only been breached in the name of the new Trinity but in the presence of the annual gathering of all Laoghaire's sub-chiefs. Swift as the wind the news would go through the forest paths and along the wild coasts. Many of the same chiefs would kneel before Patrick in the months to come and feel the oil of his anointing them bishop.

There would be other moments. He would stand on the black slated mountaintop and see the ocean that stretched endlessly to the west. One day the feet of men and women would bleed as they climbed this same Croagh Patrick in pilgrimages of faith. But Tara was God's moment and Patrick's hour.

Columba

Died 9 June AD 597

It were my soul's desire
To see the face of God;
It were my soul's desire
To rest in his abode.

It were my soul's desire
A spirit free from gloom,
It were my soul's desire
New life beyond the doom.

Grant, Lord, my soul's desire,
Deep waves of cleansing sighs,
Grant, Lord, my soul's desire,
From earthly cares to rise.

It were my soul's desire
When heaven's gate is won,
To find my soul's desire,
Clear shining like the sun.

This still my soul's desire
Whatever life afford,
To gain my soul's desire
And see thy face, O Lord. Amen.

Old Irish versified, Eleanor Hull, 1860–1935

● ● ●

The vellum pages draw the eye down toward them. Even after thirteen centuries they hint of the glorious colours and the endlessly intricate design woven in that long ago world of the sixth century. They lie under the light in a quiet room in the Royal Irish Academy in Dublin. The writing is neat, the text is that of the psalms. For centuries it has been called the *Cathach* or the *Book of the Battle.*

In an extraordinary way it is a symbol of both death and life, selfishness and self-dedication, anger and submission. Because of it many men died and many other men and women came to the Christian faith. The one who copied this script and about whom all these contrasts swirled was an Irish priest named Columba.

Born in the harsh northern reaches of the Inishown Peninsula in northern Donegal, he was rich, imperious, volatile. He did all things with a passion. As with much Celtic spirituality there was a wrestling between nobility of birth and submission to the divine will, between pride and humility, between an instinct for avenging real or imagined wrongs and the demands of Christian forgiveness.

A book was borrowed in an age when such things were few and therefore of great value. Columba returned the book, the psalter now lying in its display case thirteen centuries later, but only after he had copied it. The owner demanded the copy. Legal opinion was sought at the ultimate level of the High King at Tara. The judgement echoes down the centuries in its picturesque simplicity: "To every cow her young cow, that is her calf, and to every book its copy."

A smouldering Columba returned the copy. Within weeks, and still inside the bounds of Tara, it took only another confrontation to send Columba north to gather his tribe or clan for battle. To do battle was still quite normal for the great monastic communities which were then developing. Indeed most were merely the ancient tribal unit made Christian.

The result was an appalling death toll. For Columba it was traumatic, and his reaction was typical of his nature. Passionate rage was followed by passionate remorse and self-condemnation. The man of action in him channelled that remorse into a decision that was to change the course of Christian history. He would leave his country for ever and give the rest of his life to winning for Christ as many souls as had perished through his rage and pride. Being the kind of man he was, he had no difficulty in finding others to follow him. It was the year AD 563; Columba was forty-two years old.

• • •

It was difficult to believe that two weeks had not passed since the coastline of Inishown had dropped away into the mist and spray. They had moved down the Foyle checking the seams of the skins along the sides of the great curragh, testing the leather sail, at first responding to the shouted greeting of someone on the shore, until the estuary broadened and the only sounds were the slapping of the water and their own voices.

As he took his turn at an oar, he smiled to realize how much he had changed with time and events. He remembered the days of agonized remorse following the battle, days when he had come to realize that the proud rage that possessed him at times was the only thing still not laid on the altar of Christ. He realized that he had said the promises of humility and worn its girdle but had never embraced its reality. But now he had begun. Once he would have exhorted the monks to row, now he sat at the great oar himself feeling the rough wood making his buttocks raw and the sea tearing at the muscles of thigh and arm, forcing him to bend before the power of Mac-Nannan, ancient god of the sea. Day after day they rowed north and east commending themselves to the Christ who had stilled the storm and walked the waters. Columba was conscious of no fear. Had he not seen in a dream an island and a welcoming harbour.

The vicious winds of the eastern Atlantic took them first to a place of welcome and warmth, even in a sense to kinsmen. The mainland colony kingdom of Dalriada let them rest and gather their strength. One day far in the future the area would be called Kintyre. From there they headed to sea again, the curragh repaired, food and water replenished, their voices joining with those on the beach singing psalms until sight and sound were lost.

The dawn brought them to an island seen first as a hilltop in the wilderness of sea. Columba found his eyes devouring it. Would it be home, the end of the quest, the beginning of so many hopes. They beached the curragh, aching to get to land. He felt their surprise and resentment when he ordered them to stay while he went ahead. He knew that they were watching him as he walked among the wild grasses, crossed the meadow area, and began to climb the hillock they had first seen. At the top he turned to the southwest and stood for a long time peering into the distance. At first he could see nothing but the low clouds; then they broke for a moment and he could see a long line of dark coastline. Once again came the memory of his vow — never again to set eyes on the land where he had betrayed his Lord by his death dealing rage. He knew the disappointment showed on his face and in his voice as he directed them back into the boat. Their silence was eloquent in their disappointment and weariness. He was conscious of the possibility of testing them beyond endurance.

Hours later he saw the island. He saw it first because he had handed over the oar to another so that he could call out the wild confident verses of the Psalm 104 as encouragement for them.

O Lord, how manifold are your works!
in wisdom you have made them all;
the earth is full of your creatures.

Yonder is the great and wide sea
with its living things too many to number,
creatures both small and great.

There move the ships,
and there is that Leviathan,
which you have made for the sport of it.

I will sing to the Lord as long as I live;
I will praise my God while I have my being.

At first he thought the island was a promontory of the

mainland. As they came nearer he saw that a stretch of water about a mile wide intervened. They approached from the south to see a small harbour with rocks at its mouth and behind it little rounded hills. This time he deliberately quelled hope. The others sensing his mood were likewise silent. They pulled steadily in, carefully avoiding the jagged rocks, visibly relaxing as the sea died down and they approached the stony beach. This time they did not need the admonition to remain by the boat. Again he went forward and crossed the fields above the beach. They saw him stop before he set out to decide which hill was the highest. Reaching the summit of it he stood for a long time facing south. Finally they saw him coming back. Somehow they knew his verdict. His walk, his pace, the fact that he waved while still at a distance.

Even before he reached them they had begun to pull the curragh further up the beach. He gathered them in a circle huddled against the wind, and he lifted his voice in thanksgiving for the voyage and for the landfall. His voice rose and fell, and they could hear all the hope and plans and resolutions pour from him in a flood of lyrical utterance, such as had won him the highest of all titles in his celtic world. *Ollamh* or chief poet they knew him to be. Now on this lonely windswept island there came together all the richness of language and imagination of a thousand pagan generations, fused with the boundless treasury of spirituality found in the young Christ rising to bring back light to a darkened world. Columba ended his passionate outburst of praise, and the whole company responded with the psalm that had been the song of unnumbered pilgrims on land and sea.

I lift up my eyes to the hills;
from where is my help to come?

My help comes from the Lord,
the maker of heaven and earth.

The Lord shall watch over your going out
and your coming in,
from this time forth for evermore.

Their voices fell silent. The sounds of the sea and the wind and the crying of seabirds swept over them, reminding them of their human needs of shelter, food, and drink. They set about emptying the curragh. A few of them went to select a site that itself might afford an element of shelter. The island had as yet no name; so they referred to it merely by the word *island* which in their language was *Ioua*.

Centuries later a monk, wearying over copying the script that told the story of Columba, would make a slight error. The word would become *Iona*. By then there would have come true a prophecy implicit in a remark made by Columba on the day of their landing. One of the monks had remarked that the island was small. Columba had said, "Yes, but it shall yet be mighty."

Becket

Archbishop, Martyr, died 30 December AD 1170

Beloved, we do not think of a martyr simply as a good Christian who has been killed because he is a Christian: for that would be solely to mourn. We do not think of him simply as a good Christian who has been elevated to the company of the Saints: for that would be simply to rejoice: and neither our mourning nor our rejoicing is as the world's is. A Christian martyrdom is no accident. Saints are not made by accident. Still less is a Christian martyrdom the effect of a man's will to become a Saint, as a man by willing and contriving may become a ruler of men. . . . A martyrdom is never the design of man; for the true martyr is he who has become the instrument of God, who has lost his will in the will of God, not lost it but found it, for he has found freedom in submission to God. T.S. Eliot, Murder in the Cathedral (London: Faber and Faber, 1964).

• • •

As in any great drama the confrontation of Thomas Becket, Archbishop of Canterbury, and Henry Plantagenet, King of England, was played out on a complex of stages. There was the interior stage of their personalities as two human beings, the stage of the realm of England, and finally the stage of western Europe. The characters and the issues involved transcended their own generation. Henry and Thomas struggled in a love-hate relationship; they became not so much two human beings as two archetypes of their century. They represented too much; they carried too great a burden of significance, to remain mere individuals. Whether they realized it or not (as men rarely do in the thick of their own chapter of history) Henry and Thomas were borne irrevocably on the crest of two great tides that were coming to full flood in the twelfth century. The men who caused these tides to flow were now long dead, but only in the latter half of the twelfth century was the tide flooding.

Those of us in the twentieth century who have grown up with the bland image of the church on the corner lot, its minister gently or shrilly exhorting his flock, its pathetic and regular appeals for minimum financial support, its program of pleasant family things, see only the shadow of a former empire. Men of the twelfth century would not recognize this pathetic emasculated thing, any more than the Knights Templar, thundering eastward as Crusaders to take the holy places for God and the church, would recognize themselves today in the local branch of the Red Cross giving suburban children swimming lessons. For the essential thing to realize, if we are to understand the power struggle of Henry and Thomas, is that it was precisely that, a struggle for power, for very great stakes.

Henry and Thomas, king and archbishop, represented rival empires. And we must be quite clear that both empires were based very much in this world. Two figures of the time help drive this home. By the end of the eleventh century the church probably owned about a quarter of the land of every realm in Christendom. And at that same time, it has been reckoned, one out of every thirty adult males in western Europe was a cleric of some kind. Henry and Thomas fought a cold war. What lay at stake was nothing less than the political, cultural, and judicial possession of western Europe from the Adriatic to the Atlantic, from the Mediterranean to the Baltic.

Two roads lead to the bloody episode at the altar of Canterbury Cathedral that cold December night in 1170. On those two roads two images form and struggle again and again in the centuries that saw Europe emerge from the Dark Ages and approach the savage splendour of the early Middle Ages. One is the image of the king who also would be priest, the other of the pope who would also be emperor. Between these two images — whether the faces would be Pope

Gregory and Henry of Germany in 1076 or those of Thomas of Canterbury and Henry of England a century later — medieval society stood, pulled one way and then the other, sometimes desperately torn in its loyalty.

Between these two images stands also the medieval mind, a mingling of motivation from the crassest self-interest to the most genuine idealism. Eventually these two images of authority find their classic embodiment in the love and hatred of two men, bringing to one shame and to the other death.

• • •

The fourteenth of June in the year 1170 was a lovely day. Many thought it belied the darkness of the event all were witnessing. It was an event worth watching, even if it had to be seen through lines of men-at-arms. But it is not every day one sees a prince crowned, a young prince who looks a very worthy son of old King Henry.

And there were the bishops too, especially York in all his finery, his personal men-at-arms surrounding his huge sumptuously quilted horse, the jewels of his mitre flashing in the sun, the bells of Westminster pealing out over the city and far beyond its walls into the green countryside.

Many of the watching crowd noted that, though the occasion was festive, the faces of the illustrious participants were serious and some were even morose and fearful. Many realized the good reason for this. For what was taking place was without precedent in England's history. A crowning was being performed by a bishop other than Canterbury. The enormity of it filled men and women with a vague dread of undefinable consequence. Some felt that Pope Alexander would place the land under a dreaded interdict. Some simple folk were convinced that a blight would come on the land itself and spoil the crops, bringing hunger and death. Some said that this would force the Archbishop Thomas to lead an army against the king.

The feast of St Mary Magdalene 22 August. The fields

around the village of Fretebal in France are baking in the heat of summer. King Henry is waiting with a group of his highest nobles while an entourage of equal size moves toward them out of the nearby woods. As the visitors arrive, Henry moves forward, a gesture that surprises his companions, and salutes Thomas Becket, Archbishop of Canterbury, now long in exile from England because of his struggle with this same Henry. The two salute each other with reserve, but Henry continues to make generous gestures unusual for a king. He stands beneath Becket, plays the role of a squire as he helps the archbishop from his horse. They enter the great coloured tent set in the field. Over welcoming drink and food they try once again to find a *modus vivendi* in this struggle for power between the throne and the church. Henry promises all will be well if only Becket will return to England and Canterbury. Becket responds and asks for one more guarantee. He stands and asks the King to exchange publicly the Kiss of Peace. It is the most solemn and binding symbolic act of the age. It forms part of the action of the Mass. To give the Kiss of Peace and later to betray it is to become a Judas and therefore to be damned.

Henry refuses to give this ultimate gesture. Yet before they part Becket, realizing that he must risk trusting Henry and that complete reconciliation is probably impossible, agrees to return to Canterbury. Only days later as he arrives at Rouen he is to meet the escort promised him by Henry. As Becket's procession nears the city there rides from the gate a familiar figure surrounded by men-at-arms. It is John of Salisbury, an old and sworn enemy. Each takes refuge in formality and Becket enters Rouen.

All the way from Sandwich to Canterbury the crowds gather. They are obviously delirious with joy that the archbishop has returned. Miles before he reaches the Cathedral he hears the bells pealing. The great doors open for him and he is led to the chair of St Augustine, the shouts of the monks echoing that of the crowds outside.

But within days there is a chilled silence. Becket makes an

unsuccessful attempt to see the young Henry. The older Henry is still battling away in France. There is a flesh-crawling moment when from the heart of a London crowd a woman's high voice calls out, "Archbishop, beware of the knife." By this time Becket knows that he has already in his first week made new powerful enemies by delivering the Pope's letter of excommunication for the bishops of York, London, and Salisbury. He does not know it, but it is this last action that will trigger the martyrdom he has come to regard as inevitable. Even as he settles in again at Canterbury in his household, the three bishops have crossed the channel and are in Normandy closeted with a fuming Henry.

29 December 1170. Only a few days have passed since the fatal banquet with Henry. They had all drunk too much. They had toasted Henry, as he had them, and together they had cursed all meddling archbishops. They had suddenly seen Henry's face twist in drunken anger and maudlin self-pity. Aloud he had shouted something about being rid of Becket. No more was said. No more was needed for four knights sitting at the same table. By dawn they had left to take ship for England.

It is four in the afternoon when they clatter into the dining hall of Canterbury and face Becket. Becket's faithful chaplain Fitz-Stephen will record the conversation of the next hour. Reading it today one notes an obviously futile attempt at rational communication. On both sides reason suddenly breaks as pent up emotions are released. After the meal is over and the time for devotion nears, the archbishop moves with his monks into the Cathedral. For a while the knights are unsure what to do next. For the first time they are faced with the appalling prospect of murdering the Archbishop of All England in his own cathedral. Becket refuses to lock the door into the cathedral. There is the last moment of calm before the horror. For a few moments the voices of the community begin to rise and fall as Vespers begins. Suddenly the door is opened, armour clatters across the great nave, the voices of the monks falter, die away, and then there is general panic.

In the candlelit vault of the sanctuary only Becket and three or four monks (among them Fitz-Stephen) stand facing the knights. Obviously any attempt at communication is long gone.

In a low voice Becket begins to associate himself already with the past. He recites the list of his predecessors, some of them even by now regarded as saints in the medieval world. William de Traci aims a blow at the bent head, severing instead the arm of a monk trying to ward the blow from Becket. Blood spurts on the flagstones and suddenly it releases savagery. Becket has a moment to hurriedly whisper the classic last words of Christian martyrdom, "Into thy hands, O Lord, I commend my spirit." A moment later a blow hurtles him against the altar, half his head severed. Each of the Knights hacks at the prostrate body, the last of them deliberately with his sword scooping the brains from the open skull, and scattering them on the flags.

Within seventy-two hours Henry receives the news in Normandy. He is too appalled to reply or to react coherently. Archbishops had been killed by pagans before in the history of Europe, but here was an archbishop butchered in his own cathedral, if not on the orders of a Christian king, at least at his instigation. When it became known, it would seem to many that the whole foundation of the medieval world was disintegrating. The consequences that could flow from the deed were enough to daunt even a Plantagenet.

12 July 1174. Before a great crowd Henry publicly bares his back to be flogged by the monks of Canterbury at the tomb of the martyr Thomas Becket. The archbishop is already canonized a saint, his grave rapidly becoming a major shrine for all of Christendom.

Bonhoeffer

Pastor, Theologian, Martyr, died 23 April 1945

Who Am I?

Who am I? They often tell me
I would step from my cell's confinement
calmly, cheerfully, firmly,
like a squire from his country-house.

Who am I? They often tell me
I would talk to my warders
freely and friendly and clearly,
as though it were mine to command.

Who am I? They also tell me
I would bear the days of my misfortune
equably, smilingly, proudly,
like one accustomed to win.

Am I then really all that which other men tell of?
Or am I only what I know of myself,
restless and longing and sick, like a bird in a cage,
struggling for breath, as though hands were compressing
    my throat,
yearning for colours, for flowers, for the voices of birds,
thirsting for words of kindness, for neighbourliness,
trembling with anger at despotisms and petty humiliation,
tossing in expectation of great events,
powerlessly trembling for friends at an infinite distance,
weary and empty at praying, at thinking, at making,
faint, and ready to say farewell to it all.

Who am I? This or the other?
Am I one person today, and tomorrow another?
Am I both at once? A hypocrite before others,
and before myself a contemptibly woebegone weakling?
Or is something within me still like a beaten army

fleeing in disorder from victory already achieved?
Who am I? They mock me, these lonely questions of mine.
Whoever I am, Thou knowest, O God, I am thine.

Dietrich Bonhoeffer, Letters and Papers from Prison (London: SCM Press, 1971).

• • •

Sometime in the afternoon of 20 July 1944 an abortive attempt was made to kill Adolph Hitler. When it failed, the resulting witchhunt uncovered a very real, vital, and widespread German resistance movement that involved high-ranking army officers, local politicians, trade union officials, and German churchmen.

In 1942 during the last week of May, two German churchmen had travelled to Stockholm to meet an Englishman, George Bell, Bishop of Chichester. They asked him if he would use his position to approach Anthony Eden. He was to ask Eden if, in the event of Hitler being dealt with by the Resistance, the Allies might accept subsequent peace overtures from Germany. One of the Germans even gave Bell a list of the leading figures in the Resistance. The effort came to nothing.

One of those Germans returned to Berlin. He was suffering a peculiar agony. He had begun the war as a pacifist. Till now he had shown himself an uncompromising opponent of Hitler. Now he took the great crisis decision of conscience. Hitler was evil. He had to die. Violence was necessary. In taking that decision Dietrich Bonhoeffer, then 36 years old, pastor and theologian, not only went against all his former most deeply held beliefs, he also took the first steps to the scaffold.

In the early and middle thirties, as Hitler consolidated his power, Bonhoeffer operated from a base of pacifism. He hoped some day still to get to India to meet Mahatma Ghandi. Yet events drew him into the struggle for survival then developing in German church life.

In 1935 he was asked by the Confessing Church to lead a clandestine seminary in Finkenwalde in Pomerania, not far from Stettin. Thus would be ensured future pastors for the Confessing Church, in spite of Nazi determination to destroy it. Here in two buildings, and with the bare necessities for study or comfort, Bonhoeffer forged a generation of pastors who were to pass through the fires of the Hitler years. By November 1937 no less than twenty-seven former Finkenwalde students were in prison. By February 1938 Bonhoeffer himself was getting involved in contacts with Beck, an army general, and Admiral Canaris, all of them wishing to rid Germany of Hitler.

In 1939 some American churchmen, among them Reinhold Niebuhr, made possible for Bonhoeffer a visit to the United States. It was his second. Even though a number of commitments had been made, the visit became from the beginning a time of agonized self-questioning for him. Physically he was in America, mentally and emotionally he was in Germany. He had to choose quickly.

• • •

After supper he went for a walk in Times Square. The evening of 19 June 1939 was warm and sunny. He felt very much on his own as he walked among the various strollers. Paul Lehmann was away from New York, and his advice now as a friend would have meant everything. In the morning he was facing one of the most difficult decisions of his life. He knew that what he had to say would probably at best be accepted without understanding and at worst would create a great deal of anger. He had decided, or thought he had decided — such was his agonized frame of mind — not to stay in the United States. He would go back to Germany. Still thinking, still dreading the morning, he went back to the small room in Union Theological Seminary, wrote his diary for a while, tried to sleep, and for the most part failed.

Over three weeks ago he had sailed from Germany. The

setting out in itself was not euphoric. He could not get rid of a nagging doubt about his own motives. He had managed to delay his call up for military service. His colleagues in the small beleaguered Confessing Church had agreed that he should go if only to solicit the help of the Federal Council of Churches in the United States on their behalf. A few months before on a visit to England he had met with frustration as he tried to gain assistance from the World Council of Churches. His only hope came from a fortuitous chat with Visser't Hooft, the council's general secretary, as they both walked the platform at Victoria station in London.

Now he was in downtown New York, invited here and offered a number of possible positions, intending until today to stay for a year. Tomorrow he would be expected to inform Henry Leiper of the Federal Council of Churches of his acceptance of one position or the other, and he felt he could accept neither. Guilt about being so far away from all that was happening to friends in Germany was becoming too strong. The circle was obviously closing in on all who questioned the regime.

Such were the reasons he tried to give Leiper, and as he expected, they were not well received. It would have been better if the newspaper or letters could have given him a definite crisis to justify his decision. He wrote that night: "It is strange that I am never quite clear about the motives which underlie my decision . . . at the end of the day I can ask only that God may judge this day, and all the decisions, mercifully. It is in his hands now."

The next two days were hell. Again and again the enormity of the decision swept over him. In his diary he wrote, "We cannot separate ourselves from our destiny," almost as if he suspected where the path would lead and wished not "to drink the cup."

That evening of 22 June he wrote to Reinhold Niebuhr, the giant of American theologians. The inner conflict is obvious. "I have made a mistake in coming to America . . . . I will have no right to participate in the reconstruction of Christian life in Germany after the war if I do not share the trials of this time with my people." The next morning, 12 August, he booked a passage from New York, feeling that he simply could not renege on doing the Summer School lectures before he left.

The letter from Pomerania the next day changed everything. Goebbels had made a vicious speech in Danzig. In the same mail he heard from his brother Karl Friedrich who was in Chicago. He too was returning to Germany. Before reading the two letters Dietrich had read his daily Bible study booklet. The text was 2 Timothy 4:21, Paul's request to Timothy, "Do your best to come before winter." The two letters and the text left no doubt. He cancelled the passage for August and booked one for 8 July.

Only one more factor would give him doubts. On 30 June at long last, a letter arrived from Paul Lehmann telling him of promising responses to Paul's letter commending Bonhoeffer to various institutions. While Bonhoeffer appreciated it, he saw to his consternation a reference in the circular letter to the church community in Pomerania which would give the German authorities excuse to act punitively. He got in touch with Paul and besought him to circularize another letter saying that the reference was a mistake. It was a sad and frantic end to Lehmann's well-intentioned efforts.

The evening of 7 July was hot and humid. Almost at midnight the liner slipped her moorings and sailed from New York. Paul Lehmann had come to say good-bye. They would never see each other again.

Bonhoeffer stayed ten days with his sister in London. A letter he wrote to George Bell, Bishop of Chichester, by now an old friend, says, "It is uncertain when I shall be in this country again . . . . We shall never forget you during the coming events."

On 25 July late in the evening he left London on the boat train. Two days later he reached Berlin. The struggle with all that Hitler was would continue until the dawn of Monday 9 April 1945, when Bonhoeffer would die on the gallows in the prison at Flossenburg. Years later the doctor who saw the prisoners before execution would say, "In almost fifty years that I worked as a doctor I have hardly ever seen a man die so entirely submissive to the will of God."

Romero

Archbishop, Martyr, died 24 March 1980

Fourth Knight: *What I have to say may be put in the form of a question:* Who killed the Archbishop? *Consider the course of events. From the moment he became Archbishop, he completely reversed his policy; he showed himself to be utterly indifferent to the fate of the country, to be, in fact, a monster of egotism, a menace to society. This egotism grew upon him, until it became at last an undoubted mania. Every means that had been tried to conciliate him, to restore him to reason, had failed. He used every means of provocation; from his conduct, step by step, there can be no inference except that he had determined upon a death by martyrdom. This man, formerly a great public servant, had become a wrecker. . . .* T.S. Eliot, Murder in the Cathedral (London: Faber and Faber, 1964).

● ● ●

One of the great chasms in contemporary Christianity is the fact that, while in the developed world Christian faith is looked to primarily as personal therapy enabling men and women to deal with a daunting reality, in the underdeveloped world where Christianity is the faith of a society, it is frequently seen in terms of political and social liberation.

In such parts of the world the images and themes of the Judeo-Christian heritage that seem to have pierced to the heart of human experience are those of Exodus, with its story of a people moving from slavery even at the risk of death in the Red Sea, and images of social justice from the prophets of Israel such as Amos and Isaiah.

This is particularly true in Central and South America. Roman Catholicism, now part of that continent for centuries, is drawn daily into an inescapable agony of choice. Nowhere was the task of John Paul II more delicate than when he addressed this part of the world. Nowhere did he walk as keen a knife-edge in every word uttered. His avowed stance was that political goals cannot be the ultimate goals of Christian action yet neither can Christians ignore the absence of justice in society.

The complexity of the world places a further issue into the situation. Many Christian priests in South America, driven to despair about the failure of political processes to distribute wealth and land with greater justice, have looked to Marxism as a revolutionary political philosophy, claiming that it is legitimate to do so without betraying Christian faith as their motivation. In the face of this choice many, who are equally dedicated to bringing about a more just future, are equally as convinced that to adopt a Marxist interpretation of history is to betray the Christian faith. Moving among them are those fully committed to Marxism, both as political method and religious faith, who would readily exploit the present agonized Christian dialogue to bring about the destruction of any church role in society.

Such is the cauldron in which men and women in many places live their daily lives. Among those places is El Salvador, and until the particular day we are about to look at, among those men and women was Oscar Romero, archbishop. I am sure he would not wish to be considered a saint. He was frequently torn apart by the complexity of the moral choices he had to make. For much of his career he was a moderate; some would have said, a conservative. He died because some considered him a radical. Whatever the judgement be about such labels which we readily apply to one another, the title he finally bears is beyond them all. He died a martyr.

• • •

He had always found it easy to be alone, to travel inward, to deal with questions and doubts in the silence. In the early years this tendency to inwardness had given him an aura of aloofness. He realized now, at this quiet evening hour, how much all this had changed in the past few years. The quietness of the sacristy made him realize how little time for quietness there was these days. Yet he had come not only to accept this but to rejoice in it. His thoughts went back a few weeks to the annual priests' retreat. It had gone well. He had not been able to help contrasting it with early days in the diocese. Everything had changed. All relationships were intense now, either toward love or hatred. Sometimes he felt so terribly alone, particularly among his peers. He knew of course the complexity of the political situation, knew the knife-edge of silence and outspokenness the Papal Nuncio had to walk. His days at the Gregorian Institute had taught him the subtlety and complexity of Rome's dealing with its far-flung and infinitely varied empire.

He put on the white alb, expressing gratitude to the young sister who had had it washed for him. The thought struck him how its whiteness and simplicity contrasted with the refusal of everything else in his world to be black or white, to be simple. What was truth in this terrible slaughterhouse he and all of them lived in day by day, never knowing when a salutation was the last that one would exchange, never knowing a full night's sleep, always picking up the phone to hear a potential anonymous threat? The sister came back into the sacristy from the chapel having lit the candles. For a moment he saw their tiny flames as the door swung. He caught her eyes, and they both smiled without speaking.

Eyes and faces and voices were what had made life possible since he had become archbishop. Hands too, embracing, arms clasped, sometimes around him and his around others. The exchanging of the Peace had become so much more at Masses throughout the diocese, at least at his own Masses. In many ways the exchanged embraces were almost literally mutual protection, a mutual shielding from ever present death or torture or beating.

Wine splashed into a cruet in preparation for the Mass. He checked his watch. It was a few minuted to 6.30 and Mass time. There was an early morning Mass to which most of the off duty sisters and some patients came. Their world was just across the street in the hospital for terminal cancer patients, their order that of Divine Providence. He breakfasted with them and was indeed their pastor, intimately involved in their lives as they were in his. He had now opened himself so much to others, regarding them not as those over whom he had authority but with whom he shared suffering.

She took the wine out. He never saw it these days without its timeless connotation of blood. It was as if it did not need words of his in the prayer of consecration to become the blood of Christ. Already there was mixed with it so much blood in the streets, in the villages.

It was so ironic how life had taken him in this direction. He had become archbishop precisely because everything in his character to that point indicated him as politically conservative, safe, dependable. Indeed for a while he had continued to be critical of radical social action. He remembered some moments when he had felt himself crossing great rivers from which there was no going back. There was the meeting with some of his priests after the guns had been turned on the huge crowd of his people in the Plaza Libertad. Mass had been celebrated there in the square. He felt he could not stand back from that. The priest who had celebrated that day, Alfonso Navarro, had died, like so many others since, mysteriously murdered.

Again there was the moment three years ago when Romero had turned into the little room in Aguilares to see the body of Rutilio Grande, the local pastor. A Belgian Jesuit, Rutilio had given himself totally to try to form some structures of hope for the campesinos, the landless poor. From there the archbishop had gone into the little church where two other bodies lay under stained coverings.

He knew that bread would be in the ciborium in the tabernacle. Again symbol and actuality had merged in this land. Bread was the cry, if bread symbolized land, food, hope, and some justice. He pondered how strange it was that to pursue these things earned one so easily the charge of Marxism, as if being Christian was in itself not enough to make one struggle for these things. He wondered if those who ascribed to him and others a taste for Marx had even read the twenty-fifth chapter of Matthew's gospel, or ever heard the voice of Amos in another tiny and volatile society far away and long ago.

Together they said the vestry prayer and stepped out into the sanctuary. He moved effortlessly into the words of the new liturgy. The readings of the lectionary were shared by other voices. He found that Mass always energized him. Weariness and energy were one of the many levels of death and resurrection. Sometimes he felt a strange exaltation. He had found himself recently able to speak of death, surprised at himself as he did so. Even now he recalled that he had promised to offer this Mass as a memorial for the mother of a journalist friend.

He continued the familiar rhythm of the liturgy, feeding on its ageless meaning himself. Launching out into the canon of the Mass, he lifted the Host, and saying the words he replaced it. He was about to lift the chalice for consecration, seeing for a fleeting moment his own face in the red wine as indeed a priest often does. In that moment the bullet pierced his heart. It was 24 March 1980.

Acknowledgements

I would like to acknowledge my debt to the following authors and books.

Stewart Perowne, *Life and Times of Herod the Great* (London: Hodder and Stoughton, 1957) for the chapter on Herod.

George T. Stokes, *Ireland and the Celtic Church* (London: SPCK, 1928) for the chapters on Patrick and Columba.

George Greenaway, *The Life of Thomas Becket* (London: The Folio Society) and Arthur Bryant, *Makers of England* (Toronto: New American Library) for the chapter on Becket.

Eberhard Bethge, *Dietrich Bonhoeffer* (London: Collins, 1977) for the chapter on Bonhoeffer.

Placido Erdozain, *Archbishop Romero: Martyr of Salvador* (Maryknoll, N.Y.: Orbis Books, 1981) for the chapter on Romero.